What Lawyers Are Saying About
MARKETING THE LEGAL MIND

"A compelling and analytical roadmap to growing your law practice and a must-read for law firm leaders..."

—TIMOTHY CORCORAN, **MARTINDALE-HUBBELL**

FORMER V.P. MARKET PLANNING

"Henry Dahut's book is wonderful and thought-provoking."

—LINDA HAZELTON, CHAIR EDUCATION COMMITTEE,

LEGAL MARKETING ASSOCIATION

"This book is a must read for all lawyers. Henry Dahut really understands the art of law firm marketing."

—PERRY VISCOUNTY, **LATHAM & WATKINS LLP**,

PARTNER & CHAIR OF GLOBAL MARKETING COMMITTEE

"This is a great book...it belongs with the classics of law firm management and service marketing..."

—PM FORUM MAGAZINE, STEVE BARRETT, MARKETING STRATEGIST,

FORMER CMO OF PAUL HASTINGS

"This fascinating work combines business theory, human nature and even brain science in a compelling way.

—ARNOLD DEUTCH, M.D., **UCLA CLINICAL PROFESSOR**,

DEPARTMENT OF PSYCHIATRY AND NEUROLOGY

"Henry's book is a must read for any professional interested in excelling at law firm marketing..."

—ALEISHA GRAVIT, CMO OF **AKIN GUMP**

You may not agree with everything in this book, but you'll find yourself nodding with delight all the way through.

—MONTI REYNOLDS, ESQ.

If you manage a law firm, read this book. Dahut's insights into the evolution of firm marketing are vital for building a successful and thriving practice.

—JESSE SANTANA, ESQ.

Henry Dahut has put his finger on a significant insight: We must learn to fully understand the clients' perspective and therefore their heartfelt expectations of us.

—RITA A. KAHLENBERG, ESQ.

The challenges partners face in marketing and managing their firm are so vividly described and realistic, it's hard not to get heartburn when reading this book.

—KENNETH DRAKE, ESQ.

This man understands the unique personal and professional challenges facing our profession.

—BILL LIGHT, ESQ.

This book should be required reading in law school along with property and contracts.

—MYRON MOSKOVITZ, ESQ.

This book made me feel good to be a lawyer.

—MICHAEL ANGELOFF, ESQ

MARKETING the LEGAL MIND

A SEARCH
FOR LEADERSHIP

2014

LMG PRESS

Henry Alan Dahut

Marketing The Legal Mind
Revised Edition 2014

Hard cover first published 2004
Revised hard cover first published April 2014
Soft cover and E-book first published January 2014

ISBN: 978-0-9745126-0-0 (Hard cover)
ISBN: 978-0-9911136-0-6 (Soft cover)
ISBN: 978-0-9911136-1-3 (Kindle e-book)

Printed in the United States of America
Published by LMG Press

To Those Who Choose To Be
Healers Of Human Conflict

Note to the Reader

In my research for this book, more than one hundred lawyers, mostly partners, were interviewed nationwide. Over half of them belonged to large and established law firms. The rest were from regional firms and small practices. Early in the interview process, it became abundantly clear that if we were to have frank and open discussions concerning the lawyers' individual struggles in dealing with the many personal and professional challenges of managing and marketing their firms, we would need to ensure them total confidentiality. To this end, we promised that neither the lawyers' identities nor those of their firms would be disclosed or otherwise identified in the book. Consequently, where necessary, most of the individuals' names, and even their firms' regions and cities, were changed to ensure complete and absolute anonymity.

Contents

Acknowledgments

This book would not be possible without the willingness of so many of my legal colleagues to have frank and candid discussions about their personal and professional lives. At times our interviews touched on topics that were uncomfortable to discuss. Yet nearly all of them, to their great credit, pushed on and openly discussed their struggles in dealing with the many challenges of managing and marketing their firms.

I am also grateful for many friends inside and outside the profession of law and for the many scholars who have given me important feedback and encouragement. The material has been forming in my mind for a number of years, and many people have helped me along the way. I am grateful to them all, but here I am limited to naming only a few.

In particular, I would like to thank, in alphabetical order, the following people for their support, encouragement and generosity of thought: Stephen Albright, Michael Angeloff, Alice Barrett, Donna Beech, Stuart Berkeley, Gully Burns, Richard Chernick, Danniel Deublein, Arnold Deutch, Kenneth Drake, Paul Dubrow, Tammera Easter, John Gilligan, Frederico Grosso, Rita Ann Kahlenberg, Salman Khattack, Alan Kritzer, Lew Landau, Erica Levitt, William Light, Jonathan Maile, Lloyd Mann, Michael Michaels, Eugene Miller, Myron Moskovitz, Gregory Novotny, William Osterman, Charles Parselle, Celeste Prince, Todd Rash, William Relling, Jesse Santana, Jill Shigut, Laureen Vagonovitch, Lawrence Waldinger, and Joseph Zellmer.

For the development, design and production of this book I am also grateful to: Dunn+Associates (Kathi Dunn and Ron "Hobie" Hobart), Rowan Design (Christer S. Rowan), Michael Helms, Dan Poynter and Para Press, Danniel Deublein, Carolyn Wendt, Graffolio (Sue Knopf), and Barbara DeGennaro.

*"You don't have to fail
to become extinct;
you just need to succeed
less often."*

CHARLES DARWIN

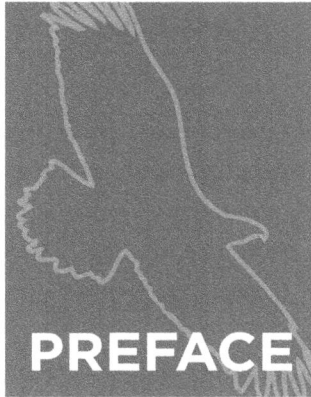

Truth In Branding
And Why It Matters

The economics of the legal market have changed considerably since the first edition of this book was published in 2004.

Over the last ten years, we have witnessed advances in law practice technology, the expanding roles of paralegals, and the outsourcing of legal work. Yet despite all of these cost-cutting and timesaving advantages, many law firms, especially the large ones, remain struggling for their very survival.

Only a decade ago, law firms were enjoying remarkable levels of growth and prosperity. Firm coffers were full and firms were spending significant sums of money on promoting themselves in order to enter new markets and acquire premium business. Some firms even began experimenting with branding.

In those days, branding was mostly viewed as just another form of advertising and promotion. In truth, firm leadership rarely understood the branding process or what the concept of branding was actually intended to accomplish. But it didn't really matter, revenue was climbing and profitability remained strong. But what so many of these firms didn't expect was that, in just a few years, our economy would be shaken by a deep and fierce recession, one which would shake the financial foundations of even the most profitable of firms.

For law firms, the recession that began in 2007 had, by 2010, penetrated the most sacred of realms—the proverbial benchmark of a firms standing and achievement—profits-per-partner.

For many firms, especially mega-firms, the decline in law partner profits were reaching record lows and it wasn't long until the legal landscape was littered with failed firms both large and small.

In an attempt to deflect further losses, firms began to lay off associates and staff in record number. But the problems went much deeper. There simply were too many lawyers and not enough premium work to go around. It was a clear case of overcapacity, and it was also clear it was not going to improve anytime soon.

More than twelve of the nation's major law firms, with more than 1,000 partners between them, had completely failed in a span of about seven years. Against this background, law schools were still churning out thousands of eager law graduates every year. Highly trained young men and women who were starved for the chance to enter a profession that once held the promise of wealth, status and stability.

As partner profits dwindled, partner infighting grew rampant. Partner would compete against partner for the same piece of business. The collegial "team-driven" identity and "progressive culture" that firms spent millions of dollars promoting as their firm's unique brand and culture had vanished as quickly as it was created.

While financial times were tough, in truth many of the big firms had the resources to survive the downturn. Instead, partners with big books of business were choosing to take what they could and joined other firms—demoralizing those left behind.

To understand why this was happening, we must first remove ourselves from the specific context and internal politics of any one firm and consider the larger picture.

The failure and decline of firms was not only a crisis of economics and overcapacity, it was also a crisis of character, identity, values and leadership.

Sadly, the brand identity many of these firms pronounced as their own did not match up against the reality of who they actually were. In other words, for many firms, the brand identity they created was illusory—and illusory brands ultimately fracture in times of financial stress and instability.

The branding process, which I refer to in the book as "firm sculpturing," was all too often viewed by firm leadership as just another clever form of market positioning, a process by which the firm created a compelling identity and then leveraged that identity against its competitors. Whether or not that identity was truthful was not really a matter of great concern.

While firms were branding and promoting themselves as dedicated, client-centric, congenial, team players, collaborative, principled, honorable, honest and forward thinking—in short, as a firm driven by its cherished beliefs and core values—in truth that brand identity rarely matched-up against the real identity. And not surprisingly, everyone inside and outside the firm knew it.

In the language of marketing, you could say it was a case of brand misidentification. In the language of psychology, it resembled a form of neurosis, disassociation and, ultimately, a profound detachment from reality.

Ultimately, the branding process must also be a *transformative process* in search of the firms highest and most cherished values. It is, and must be, a process of reinvention at every level of the firm—especially its leadership.

The transformative process is fundamental to building a true and enduring brand. Without it, firms run the risk of communicating an identity that does not represent them, and this is the danger, especially when the firm is tested against the stress of difficult times.

How this miscommunication of identity was allowed to happen varied widely from firm to firm. But generally speaking, while firm leadership was initially supportive of the branding process, in most cases these same partners were rarely willing to risk exposing the firm's real problems in fear that it would expose their own.

While decline of law firm revenue was clearly attributable to both a bad economy and an oversupply of lawyers, from an internal perspective the firm's inability to come together and develop effective measures to withstand these pressures could usually be traced directly back to the lack of partner leadership.

A firm that proclaims to be something it is not—is inevitably doomed to failure. Say nothing of the psychic damage it causes at the collective level of the firm. It is no different then the psychological dynamics of the individual who pretends to be someone he is not—ultimately it leads to confusion, frustration and eventually self-betrayal.

It's easy to indulge in self-praise when economic times are good. Some partners might even attribute their success to all that clever branding they put into place years before. But, when the threat of financial crisis enters the picture, the same firm can quickly devolve into self-predatory behavior—a vicious cycle of fear and greed that inevitably turns into an "eat-or-be-eaten" culture—which for most firms marks the beginning of the end.

For any firm playing out its last inning, it is simply too late to rally the troops or reach for those so-called cherished values that were supposedly driving the firm's success. In truth, when times got bad, these values were nowhere to be found, except on the firms website, magazine ads and brochures.

The point is that when a firm is *actually* driven by its cherished beliefs and core values, the firm will begin to live by them, especially in times of adversity. The firm will pull together and rally behind its leadership, and with clarity of purpose, each person will do what needs to be done to weather the storm.

But when there exists a fundamental contradiction between what a firm says they are, and how they actually conduct themselves both internally and to the world—the vendors with whom they do business and the clients they represent—the firm will never reach its full potential. It will remain dysfunctional and it will risk joining that growing list of failed firms.

In 2004, when I first wrote about the growing gap between promoted values versus actual values, I did not fully appreciate the degree of damage it was capable of inflicting on firms. The financial collapse and deterioration of so many law firms in the past few years is a compelling testament to the importance of insisting on truth and integrity in the branding process.

In 2014, it is clear that business-as-usual in our profession is no longer a sustainable proposition. For this reason I am convinced that firms driven by fear and greed are firms destined to eventually self-destruct. That is because, no matter how much these firms try to brand, they will never be able to brand *truthfully*, and therefore they will never be able to compete against more progressive and enlightened firms—those that do not worship wealth and power, but rather cherish personal and professional fulfillment.

There is a choice for those who believe their firm is worth saving—reinvent yourself to reflect values that are truly worthy of cherishing, or risk devolving into something less then what you aspire to be and risk your firm's soul in the process.

***

Finally, and this should come as no surprise by now, this book is not just another practice development book. Nor is it another "how-to" manual. It won't tell you how to publish more effective newsletters or develop better brochures and websites. It does not promise to make marketing fast or easy, nor does it promise instant results.

There is no simple checklist to follow and there are no breakthrough marketing technologies to share. In fact, it offers little of what you might expect from a book about law firm marketing.

Yet, if you read this book with an open mind and a true willingness to reinvent your organization, it has the power to transform your firm and make it soar.

The process of becoming something new requires courage, perseverance and, most importantly, a great deal of honest self-reflection. I believe Albert Einstein was exactly on point when he wrote about personal transformation: "I must be willing to give up what I am in order to become what I wish to be."

I hope this book will persuade you that those words are true not just for individuals, but also for professional service organizations that strive to become giants in the markets they serve.

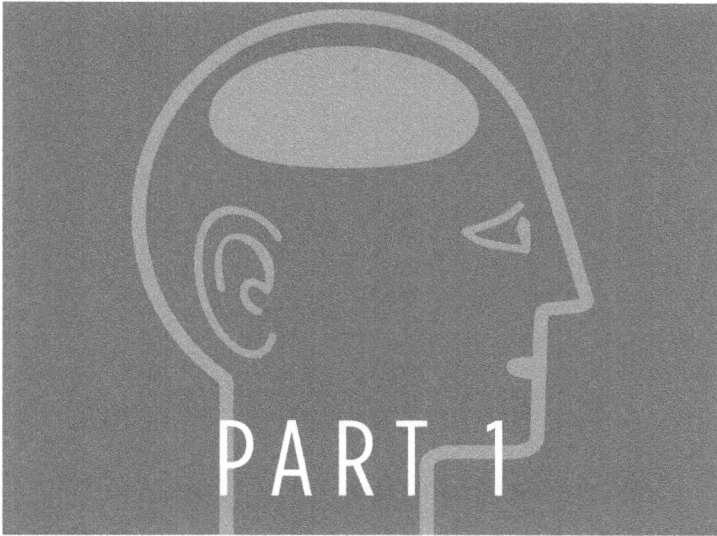

PART 1

Paid to Think

*"The basic difference between
an ordinary man and a warrior
is that a warrior takes everything
as a challenge while an ordinary man
takes everything as a blessing or a curse."*

CARLOS CASTANEDA

The Challenge

In over twenty years of working with lawyers, I have come to know many extraordinary people. Most are highly intelligent, ambitious men and women who have experienced great success in their specialty fields, yet many have struggled with the business side of their practices.

Not surprisingly, the types of problems lawyers face in *marketing* are the same types of problems they face in *managing* their practices. In a way, the two are inextricably connected. As a general rule, I found that those who were masterful in marketing their practices were also masterful in managing them.

The relationship between marketing and management is no coincidence. Marketing is a highly dynamic activity that requires focused and engaged management. It also demands that firms adopt a unified approach in seeing their practice within the context of its operational totality.

As best-selling author and business guru Theodore Levitt writes:

Marketing is not just a business function;
it's a consolidated view of your entire business process.

Understood this way, marketing need not be relegated to the single goal of client acquisition; instead it can be the foundation and driving force behind the firm's entire business—all of which can be expressed through its management, culture and leadership.

As you will learn, expanding your perspectives on marketing also means expanding the range of available business opportunities.

First, however, let's take a candid look at some of the personal and professional challenges lawyers face in trying to manage the marketing side of their practice.

Sharing the Pain

Much of the frustration lawyers have shared with me comes from being unable to shape or meaningfully direct their firms' futures. Practicing law is, in itself, demanding. Between the dual frustrations of managing and marketing a practice, most lawyers said their despair had grown exponentially.

Even the smartest, most hardworking and focused among them felt helpless when it came to charting and managing the course of their firms' future.

Carl Reed, a product liability lawyer, described the surprising disparity between his confidence and success in court and his uncertainty and anxiety about directing the course of his firm.

> *As a trial lawyer, I can actually visualize how my case will unfold. I can anticipate the depositions I'll need to take, the theme I'll develop. I know the settlement value of the case within three percentage points. Yet when it comes to managing my firm, I don't have a clue where I'm going. There's simply no plan. It's like we're on cruise control, but no one has bothered to check where we're heading. So I keep on doing what I know how to do and hope no one notices. I'm shooting for early retirement and betting I can get there before the gravy train ends.*

20

Bob Martin, a senior partner in a well-respected insurance defense firm, discussed his frustration.

> *The managing partner left the firm three years ago. I was next in line.*
>
> *I inherited a ship without a captain. This was always his firm. He brought in the business and we did the work. Our billable hours have been declining slowly. We don't dare raise our hourly rate. We desperately need to find new practice areas, but no one is taking the initiative.*
>
> *I'm in the office at seven-thirty in the morning and usually work till eight at night. There is never enough time.*
>
> *I don't dare spend too much on firm marketing. If I'm lucky, I get home in time to see my kids. My wife is used to it. We have an unwritten rule that we don't talk about my work. I don't even want to think about it. I don't run my firm. My firm runs me. Every year I promise it will be different. I've lost touch with what's really important to me. I'm so financially vested in my firm that I don't dare leave now.*

Tim Engler, a partner in a commercial litigation firm, talked about his frustration with managing the practice and the increasing level of apathy at his firm.

> *Manage and market? I don't have the time. I'm doing too much of the work! Every time I hand off a file to an associate, I end up spending more time supervising the work than I would have spent had I done it myself. I demand a quality work product. I won't put out junk. It is so hard today to find lawyers who care about the firm. All they're interested in is getting a paycheck.*
>
> *Weeks go by and I don't even know what I accomplished for myself. Sometimes I wonder if I'm doing what I really want. I*

really don't feel satisfied inside. It's like the candle burned out
before I was ready.

Finally, a very prosperous and successful managing partner had these discouraging words to say about his firm's leadership:

As I see it, one of my main goals as a managing partner is
to keep the level of discontent of the rest of my partners to a
manageable level.

Business of Law

In over one hundred partner interviews in more than twenty cities, nearly eight out of ten partners I spoke with cited the "business of law" as the most frustrating part of their practice, and more often than not, it was the area of marketing that drove them to despair.

Low morale and enthusiasm were common. Despite the financial rewards, more than half disliked the responsibilities that came with being a partner. When asked about their firm's long-term goals and how they planned to reach them, few could articulate a specific plan. Most said they would rather be left alone to practice law and let others do the managing and marketing.

"Marketing goals?" said a partner at a prominent New York firm. "You must be joking! Our idea of marketing is handing out expensive brochures at seminars that put people to sleep."

As a general rule, most partners could neither describe how their firm went about setting marketing goals nor explain how they might reach those goals. Less than half said they took a "primary role" in shaping and managing their firm's business goals.

Not surprisingly, most associates felt disconnected from firm marketing as well. Most associates had only a vague sense of what marketing meant at their firm. Some saw being involved with marketing as a rite of passage to making partner. Others said marketing meant entertaining clients. One glib associate said, "Marketing is what partners do when they renew their country club dues."

Both junior and senior associates knew they were expected to bring in new business, but they felt that they were on their own to figure out the details. For associates keen to make partner, this type of marketing is no laughing matter. They know that a mid-level associate who plays it smart can become a "made man"—to borrow an underworld term—if he can bring the right kind of client into the firm's fold, because doing so shows staying power and the ability to make rain.

Legal Skills vs. Marketing Skills

Interestingly, when partners were asked what it means to be *masterful at practicing law*, there was a great deal of consensus and no one grappled for words. Most said it took committed work, education, years of experience and, most importantly, a sincere desire to learn.

"You must be fully committed to practicing law," said a senior partner at a San Francisco firm. "It is a process. There is a very steep learning curve in the early phase. You can't let the fear of making mistakes stop you. You need a thick skin. Mistakes happen, so you can't dwell on them. The key is to learn from your mistakes. To really study them, as if your professional life depended on it."

In contrast, when partners were asked what it means to be *masterful at marketing*, there was little consensus. Some said it took "persistence and hustle," while others suggested salesmanship and people skills.

When asked how their firm went about the process of marketing, some spoke of websites, brochures, seminars and public relations. Others interpreted "marketing" to mean advertising and mentioned the Internet, television and radio.

"Practice development is just a nice way of saying marketing," said Sharon Cooper, a partner at a business litigation firm. "Marketing is just a nice way of saying sales. It's convincing people you could do a better job than the next person."

Partners had varying ideas on what marketing included. They agreed, however, that marketing was both frustrating and difficult to manage.

Service

At the end of each interview, I asked the partners whether they thought providing "excellent service" was an important aspect of the firm's marketing. Almost all responded that marketing, indeed, was about providing clients with "excellent service." But the concept was always an afterthought. Only a handful of partners mentioned it until I brought it up.

Even after the subject was raised, less than 10 percent of the partners could provide a working definition of what service meant at their own firm. But they were even less clear about what service might mean to their clients.

When I asked these senior partners what distinguished their firms from the rest—what characteristics might offer their clients an incentive to stay—the most common responses were these:

We work hard for our clients.

We're very aggressive.

We handle very big cases.

We're a national firm/a statewide firm/a local firm.

All of these are good answers—if this is what clients want. But the evidence indicates that what clients care about most—what makes them choose one firm over another—is service.

It was obvious that *service* was not at the forefront of the partners' minds. Yet, as we will see, the essence of marketing comes from defining and measuring all aspects of service within the specific context of the clients' needs and wants.

For the small percentage of firms that understand this reality, there is no ambiguity. Indeed, providing clients with excellent service is what drives these very successful firms.

"We live or die by the quality of service we deliver to our clients," said Norman Bollinger, managing partner of a highly successful Northwest firm.

"There is no magic to it. You sit and really listen to what your clients want from you. Mostly, they want you to know them—their business and

24

their challenges. I'm convinced that, first and foremost, our firm is in the people business and, to that end, we practice law."

Without service taking on a specific and defined role within the firm, it cannot be an organizing principle around which the *business* of law is conducted.

Indeed, most of marketing is about providing superior service within the context of the client's specific needs and wants. Placing anything before this—including four-color brochures, Flash-animated Web sites, public relations or promotion of any significance—is putting the cart before the horse—way before the horse! And it is the primary reason most firms' marketing programs fail before they ever get started.

Brochures, no matter how impressive, are meaningless if they don't represent the true nature of the firm. However, brochures and most other forms of promotion can be incredibly powerful—*if what you say comes from what you really are*. Indeed, nothing is more compelling and refreshing than the truth, especially when it comes from the legal profession.

The Client's Point of View

Clients want their lawyers to earn their business, which often translates into first earning their trust and respect. Clients will trust and respect a lawyer who not only protects them and stands up for their rights but also is a confidant and trusted ally.

In law school, we were taught that ultimately lawyers were *paid to think*. The left-brain analytical skills we would employ when arguing a case or writing a brief were the most important service we could offer our clients. This is true in part. But in today's market, clients want and expect much more.

In a recent interview, Gregory Haas, the CEO of a large telecommunications company in the Midwest, expressed the same sentiment: "I want a lawyer to help me think through the problems," he said. "But he must also take the time and effort to learn about my business and to understand the challenges we face in the marketplace. I want a lawyer who will have the courage to talk straight to me. And when things get tough, I need to know this person is both prepared and committed to help us through the storm." It's not uncommon for lawyers to argue that what distinguishes one firm from another *should be* its legal expertise—the quality of its work. The reality, however, is that most clients *assume* their lawyers possess the requisite experience and technical skills to effectively and competently represent them. They *assume* the legal work will be performed in a timely, professional manner. That's just the price of entry.

Clients not only assume that these professional services will be provided, but they also *want* certain other things from their lawyers. Clients *want* their phone calls to be returned promptly. They *want* promises kept. They *want* to be kept informed. They want their lawyer to help them understand the issues. And perhaps most importantly, clients *want* to be respected.

So what distinguishes one lawyer from another? It comes down to *service*. Defining service, however, is not easy, because so much depends on the needs and wants of particular clients. Defining service from the client's viewpoint rather than the lawyer's is just the starting point. Turning the notion of service into a pervasive reality within your firm is an entirely different matter.

Turning quality service into a reality in a firm means transforming the firm's culture and values at every level. It means setting greater standards of performance for everyone in the firm—not just the lawyers. It also means learning to think in new ways.

Thinking in Domains

There are many different ways to think. The way we acquire and interpret knowledge can be understood in terms of specific and discrete domains. Each of us, from computer scientists to musicians, architects, psychologists, lawyers and professional athletes, acquires and interprets knowledge differently.

People think and interpret information within the confines of their respective knowledge systems—their own *domains*. Each domain contains its own language, symbols, beliefs, rules and systems of notation. And each domain contains an interpretive construction through which people view the world.

Domains are like cultures. They provide us with both systems of knowledge and specific ways of interacting with that knowledge. Psychologist, teacher and best-selling author Mihaly Csikszentmihalyi writes:

> *Knowledge is bundled up into discrete domains—geometry, music, religion, legal systems and so on. Each domain is made up of its own symbolic elements, its own rules, and generally has its own system of notation. In many ways, each domain describes an isolated little world in which a person can think and act with clarity and concentration... Each domain expands the limitations of individuality and enlarges our sensitivity and ability to relate to the world.*

Csikszentmihalyi argues that it is not uncommon for people to spend most of their adult lives within the confines of their own domain, never stepping beyond its boundaries. For most of us, however, domains are primarily ways to make a living. We are taught early on to pursue our chosen field. For some of us, this was the field of law.

Outside of the specific content of legal knowledge that we learn, we are also taught to think logically and are given a specific point of view with which we look to the past to find solutions. We are also taught to be defensive and skeptical. For lawyers, the glass must always appear half empty.

The domain of enterprise building is very different from the domain of practicing law. The type of thinking that makes a great legal practitioner can be precisely the factor that undermines that same practitioner's success at marketing a firm and building it into a thriving enterprise.

To be an enterprise builder, you can't *think* like a lawyer. If you want to build an enterprise, you must think like an enterprise builder. This requires learning a new mind-set and having a willingness to enter the realm of new domains.

Those who can transition between different domains often have the ability to become dynamic and effective leaders because they possess what is later described in this book as *perspective-based* leadership skills. Such skills enable a person to understand and act upon the perspectives of others while knowing how to gain support for their own ideas and views through the eyes and minds of others.

A perspective-based leader is usually a highly effective manager and is often the ideal person to lead your firm from the stale marketing practices of the past to thinking about marketing in entirely new ways.

Change at this level requires a willingness to leave the comfort of one's domain and dare to imagine how things might be. Such courage will be the very catalyst of your firm's success. It will align your firm with its highest values and distinguish it from all the rest.

Examination and Discovery

True marketing is founded not just on understanding what the client needs and wants; it also requires that you engage in a meaningful inquiry as to what the *firm* needs and wants. Some have suggested that these interests may not always be compatible. This is a good point, but it should not stop the inquiry. In fact, it should move it forward.

Consider that the first inquiry (what the client needs and wants) points your examination outward, while the second (what the firm needs and wants) points your examination inward. Both perspectives are essential to the process of examination and discovery, and both contribute to forming a consolidated view of your firm's entire business process.

Understood in this context, perspective-based marketing is a way to redefine your firm's identity through the eyes of your clients. Effectively managed, this type of examination and discovery process can lead to transforming your firm into a marketing powerhouse.

However, fundamental change at this level can only emerge out of the *inspired values* that most deeply reflect the firm's leadership. Marketing that does not reflect these values will never ring true, but marketing that does will find expression at every level of the firm—from the decor in the lobby to the quality of the firm's work product.

Marketing is more about identifying firm values than it is about coming up with bigger ads and smarter slogans. Marketing works best when there is no separation—no inconsistency—between what a firm says it is and how it actually goes about its business. Marketing should dictate the experience people have of the firm. It should shape people's perceptions of the firm. It should describe the ways in which the firm holds itself accountable—not only to its clients, but also to its employees, partners and all those who do business with the firm.

This type of marketing requires a willingness to try on different perspectives—different ways of thinking. Some say this is contrary to how lawyers have been trained to think. Lawyers are said to be too rigid in their thinking— too linear in their logic to be able to think differently. I do not agree. Lawyers are knowledge-based professionals who are fully capable of shifting perspective and considering differing points of view.

One of the keys to mastering marketing is to be open to using a different type of thinking from that used when practicing law. The linear logic with which lawyers practice law must give way to alternate perspectives when they think in the domains of marketing and enterprise building. When lawyers are able to change their thinking, new and exciting possibilities emerge.

At a personal level, this new approach calls on us to ask how different our professional lives would be if we could work toward goals we deeply value— if we could hold a vision of these values in our mind and create ways of incorporating them into the fabric of the workplace. Viewing marketing from this perspective encourages us to measure how well we transform these values into our professional lives.

2

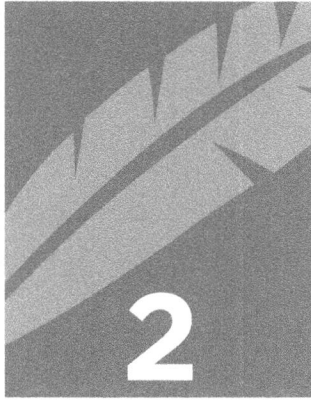

The Client Experience

Receiving exceptional service is always a memorable experience. It can make a person feel valued. And news of exceptional service spreads fast. It's talked about to friends and family and even eulogized to strangers. It can transcend the ordinary and take on an almost mythical form. This is especially true when ordinary things are done in extraordinary ways.

Years ago, I had to fly to Bangkok on a business trip. After a long, trying taxi ride in rush-hour traffic, I finally checked into my hotel, tired and hungry. I dropped my luggage in the room and went downstairs to get some dinner. An hour later, when I returned, I found my luggage neatly unpacked—shirts folded, pants hung up, ties carefully dispersed along the racks. Almost immediately, I began to relax. I involuntarily breathed a sigh of relief.

Then I looked into the bathroom and saw something I'll never forget. The items from my overnight kit had been neatly arranged by the sink, and someone had actually cleaned my hairbrush. All of the hair strands had been removed and the bristles were glistening. But the *coup de grace* was this: Resting in the center of the bristles was a beautiful white petal.

After more than ten years, I can still see this image. This one experience— this unexpected gesture that went beyond exceptional service—left me with a whole new understanding of what it means to put a client first.

When I returned home and people asked about Thailand, I invariably told them about that small white petal on my hairbrush. Today, when I think of great hotels, I think of the Hotel Oriental. It is the standard by which I judge all other hotels.

In the universe of companies, only a few consistently reach extraordinary levels of service. Studies have shown that companies that *do* reach such levels share certain fundamental values and organizational traits.

Marketing a Service

There is a fundamental distinction between marketing a *product* and marketing a *service*. Products are tangible. They either work as represented or they don't. Products can be returned or exchanged. We can touch and feel a product before we decide to buy it; rarely is this the case with a service.

Services are meant to be experienced, not ordered from catalogs. Services are profoundly personal in nature and our response to them is often emotionally driven. A service relationship, especially a *professional* service relationship, challenges the provider to be an expert in serving people.

Think about the ways buyers perceive "value" generally. When we buy products, we rely mostly on *objective* criteria. For products like shampoo and stereos, determining objective value is fairly simple. A large bottle of shampoo delivers more product than a small one, so we are justified in paying more for the large one. A stereo system that has more features is said to contain more value than one that has fewer features. Product features, quality and quantity are all critical factors in the determination of value. Service, however, is far more nebulous—and is therefore much more challenging to define and measure.

Service Is a Process, Not an End

One reason service is so difficult to measure is because it's so subjective. It is *experiential*—we can feel it and see it, but defining it is another matter.

Perhaps it's a little like what the Supreme Court wrote about pornography: *It may be hard to define, but we know it when we see it...*

Truly great firms—those with legendary status—are always striving to reach greater levels of service for their clients. Fundamental to such firms is the understanding that service is a never-ending *process* driven by a specific mind-set. These firms know that while they must always try to reach higher levels of service, they can never assume they have achieved the *highest* level. There is always a higher level to strive for, and standing still squelches the pursuit of excellence. Either a firm continues to reach for higher service levels or it has abandoned the pursuit. There is no middle ground.

Most firms revolve around the desires and needs of their partners. For service-driven firms, just the opposite is true—not because these firms have partners who enjoy a higher sense of purpose, but because they have a higher sense of business smarts. For them, everything revolves around the client. And as you might expect, the benefits have a way of coming back to the partners. Consistently delivering increasingly higher levels of service to clients builds the types of returns that keep a firm thriving.

There is no quick and easy recipe for becoming a service-driven firm. There is no secret formula for meeting—and exceeding—your clients' needs. But one of the best ways to find out how your firm can provide exceptional service for your clients is, strangely enough, one of the most frequently ignored: *listening* to what your clients need—being *client-centric* instead of *firm-centric.*

You may be convinced that your best clients have been attracted by the stature of your firm—by its size or its range of specialties. But the truth is that it's not what you *think* you're offering that counts, but rather what the clients are *experiencing* that matters most.

Any time you have a chance to determine what your clients need and want from you, consider it a priceless opportunity to learn. Their needs and wants—and their experience with your firm—are the key to identifying the focus of your marketing efforts. Finding and delivering what your clients need and want will not only result in satisfied clients but, if you apply this knowledge to your practice, their experience of your firm can also become your branding.

At a corporate law firm in Century City a few years ago, a senior partner shook hands with one of his clients after completing the company's first public offering. The two men reminisced about their long relationship. "We've been through a lot together—both good and bad—from climbing out of our financial mess, to the opening of our first four stores, to building out nearly four hundred of them, to finally going public," the president of the company said, smiling. "It wasn't an easy journey, but I'm sure glad in the end that it was you who was with us. No matter where we were, you were always there too."

When a client speaks to you from the heart, the insight you receive will be priceless. The marketing materials for that Century City law firm had previously emphasized their track record, their versatility and their willingness to be tough. Had they failed to incorporate this client's insight, they would have missed a precious marketing opportunity. Luckily, the senior partner was a savvy marketer. He immediately knew the value of a long-term client's praise. It became an important part of the firm's identity and, after a while, made its way into the firm's branding and marketing material: "Wherever you go, that's where we'll be…"

Beyond the decent service, the sound legal advice and the expectation of professionalism, what mattered to that client on an emotional level was that this firm had been by his company's side through the good times and the bad.

Not all of your clients will hand you a resonant marketing phrase. But an experienced marketing professional with the proper skills can make you more aware of them when this does happen, and more importantly, can help you use them to shape the way your firm brands its services. But the key in this example is not the catchy phrase or even the kind expression of gratitude. What makes the Century City firm's marketing insight so important is the fact that it represents a *fundamental truth* about the firm: It *does* stick by its clients even when times get rough. That's how the firm does business.

In the late 1990s, one of the largest law firms in the nation decided it wanted to tap into the technology boom. The marketing team advised the firm to target small start-up companies and offer them a reduced hourly rate for general business matters in the hope that, if the business succeeded, the firm would be handed all their legal work, including taking them public. The marketers believed that doing this would demonstrate the firm's commitment and loyalty to their smaller, more vulnerable clients. One such client had this unfortunate experience dealing with the firm:

> *In the beginning, the firm really seemed interested in what we were trying to create. They spent time getting to know us and expressed a real desire in seeing us succeed. I really believed them. I was invited to firm-sponsored seminars and even got invited to the firm's sky booth for the big game. Everything was going well until the technology bubble burst—and with it, our close relationship with the firm. No more friendly partner calls to see how we were doing. After a while, I was lucky to get my calls returned. They knew we were strapped for cash and, when we were unable to pay their bills, they sued us. They didn't just sue the corporation (the one they helped us set up), they sued me personally, since I was the president of the company. It was a disaster. When the chips were down, this firm came at us with knives. I will never forget this experience—nor will my associates and friends.*

It doesn't take a marketing genius to know that it's bad business to sue your clients, but the contrast between the Century City firm and this one is worth noting. One firm made a loyal friend out of a client while the other made an enemy. The point is that how a firm does business, whether it's how they manage their receivables or which new practice group they decide to open, says something important about the firm in relationship to its clients.

In most cases, firms consider internal business decisions to be entirely internal—separate and distinct from the external side that the public sees. Firms fail to recognize that what a firm *is* can often be measured by the decisions it makes, and they often make decisions without regard to the effect they might have on clients, even in indirect ways. Firms must consider the ways in which their decisions may change the nature of the contact between them and their clients.

Law firms make important business decisions every day, and rarely do they consider the impact on those who do business with the firm. When problems do surface, they are often handed over to the public relations department to clean up.

The Zone of Contact

Consider that almost everything a firm does or communicates impacts the clients' experience of the firm. The parts of a firm that clients deal with directly are part of the firm's *zone of contact.*

Everything a firm does is, in some way, an expression of the firm's values or lack of values. Every act or omission reveals the level of the firm's commitment or lack of commitment.

Everything—from the paper stock the firm uses to its policy of returning phone calls to how lawyers and staff greet new clients and say good-bye to departing ones—can impact clients. Even small things—like the quality of coffee, the effort put forth to make a client feel welcomed, the demeanor of a law clerk and the pictures on the wall can make a difference.

Sophisticated marketing experts take great effort and time in examining a firm's major points of contact. The quality of the client's satisfaction relative to a particular point of contact is an indicator of the general health of the firm. Much of marketing consists of translating these ordinary points of contact and shaping them into positive client experiences.

Altering the point of contact to be more in line with the client's satisfaction will certainly improve the quality of the service your firm provides, but it will not, by itself, bring about a fundamental change in the firm's quality of service. For this, the firm must examine its innermost core—the primary leadership and the inspired principles these leaders rely on when building the firm's character. Only by reaching this level can you transform your firm from ordinary to extraordinary.

Figure 2.1 illustrates how most firms go about improving the quality of their service. They make superficial changes—quick fixes—at external contact points. The problem, of course, is that a quick fix cannot endure the test of time and eventually fails.

Contact points are only as good as the quality of service that speaks through them. Service must be a direct expression of the firm's values, made real through the language and actions of the entire firm. When a firm's actions are an expression of its inspired values, every point of contact becomes an expression of its unique brand of service. But the concept of service must originate from the center of the inspired values formulated by the firm's top leadership. I call these central values the firm's "V" spot. When a firm has a solid set of inspired values, every point of contact will resonate with the firm's vision.

FIGURE 2.1: External fixes and changes.

SYSTEMS · STRUCTURES · LANGUAGE · ACTION
LAWYERS & STAFF
FIRM'S LEADERSHIP
INSPIRED VALUES
V
THE FIRM'S IDENTITY

Without the formulation of inspired values and the clarity of purpose these values create, the firm will be unable to build the language, the structure and the systems necessary to ensure that all of its actions and communications are commensurate with these values.

Every action a firm takes must reflect its true identity and its inspired values; otherwise, it risks seriously damaging its reputation and its credibility.

What the firm does, what it stands for, and the promises it makes and keeps must be seen and experienced by everyone—not just clients—as an authentic expression of the firm's true identity. Only then can the inspired values become a central part of the firm's branding—the firm's persona— an undeniable statement of what the firm stands for and what people can expect of the firm, whether they're a client or a foe.

Identifying every point of contact with a client or a prospective client must become the focus of the firm's marketing efforts. Each point within the zone of contact must reflect, and be consistent with, the firm's character. A client's contact with the firm should be viewed as an opportunity to convey what it means to do business with the firm.

Assuming that the firm has taken the time to do the planning and hard work necessary to identify their inspired values, the next challenge is to ensure that everything the firm does is an accurate and sincere expression of these values—that these values are conveyed to clients and others who interact with the firm through the zone of contact.

The zone of contact is where the firm interfaces with its clients, either directly or indirectly. Since every contact the firm has with others conveys information about the firm, every contact becomes an important representation of the firm's values. The zone of contact includes everything— including the firm's business cards, the lobby decor, the receptionist, and meetings with staff, associates, lawyers and partners.

In order to maintain quality control over client satisfaction levels, many marketing professionals focus on reactions of clients to various parts of the zone of contact to make sure that what people experience in their contact with the firm is an accurate and positive expression of the firm's character.

This examination of quality focuses not on what the firm *intends* to convey as much as on the client's *actual experience* within the zone of contact. To perform such an examination, the firm must assess its major points of contact with clients, and once these contact points are identified it must determine which of the contact points elicit positive service experiences from the client.

Ideally, the specific action and communication responsible for a positive service experience can be traced to one of the firm's fundamental values. If the client is having an experience—even a positive one—that is not in keeping with the firm's values, the firm may wish to consider whether the value being conveyed is at odds with the firm's values. If it is, the firm's actions should be changed to reflect its values more accurately. If the experience is *not* at odds with the firm's values, the firm's action may simply reflect an unidentified value.

When a point of contact is in keeping with the firm's fundamental values but elicits a *negative* service experience, the challenge is to quickly determine what has gone wrong. Has an action or communication been missed? Can the firm remove a barrier between its fundamental service values and the client's experience to make the experience a more positive one? Often, what is missing is a value that is either hidden from view or unable to be expressed.

As you're no doubt beginning to see, the zone of contact is not separate from the firm—it *is* the firm, as illustrated in Figure 2.2 (see next page). The firm constantly radiates its values to clients, prospective clients, the legal community, and vendors and the business community.

When you can achieve an alignment among the inspired values of your firm, the language of your firm and the actions of your firm, marketing becomes an expression of your firm's unique identity. It becomes proprietary and is evidenced in every point of contact you have with your clients, whether the contact occurs through the legal services you provide or the way your receptionist greets the firm's visitors.

Some contact points exist quite naturally within a firm. Clients' initial calls, their first meeting, the letters and messages they receive during the course of the relationship—all of these are points of contact, and all of them ultimately become expressions of your firm's unique brand of service.

But there is no reason to leave it at that. Considering the importance of heightening the value of these contact points with clients, the firm that is determined to provide great service will create *new* points of contact. These moments allow you to meaningfully shape client interaction, making special efforts to convey the inspired values of your firm while learning more about how you can improve the quality of your service.

Instituting a completion ritual with your clients is one example of this approach. In most law firms, when a case is concluded, the client's next point of contact with the firm is the bill. For the client it's anticlimactic, to say the least. And, socially, it's counterintuitive. If you have a friend over to dinner, you shake hands at the end of the evening and say, "It's been

FIGURE 2.2: Those who make contact with the firm must see that contact as a positive experience.

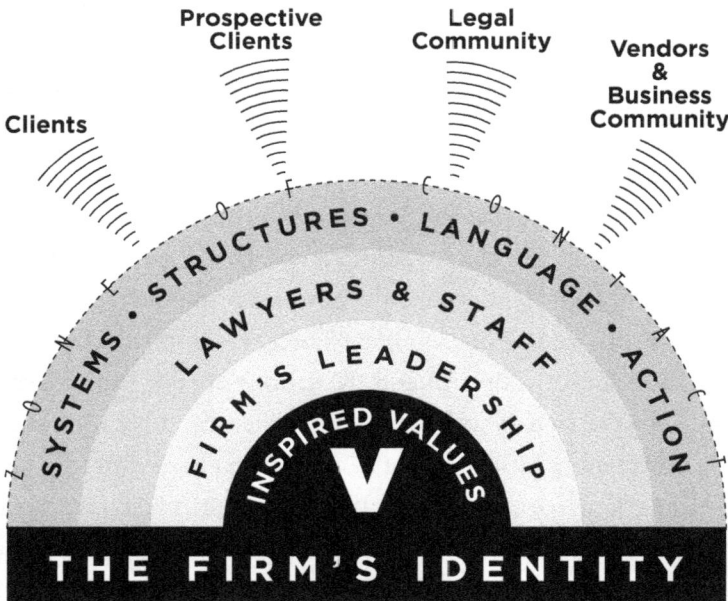

great having you here." This is a social nicety that provides a tiny ritual of completion. Clients, in contrast, are typically left dangling.

Imagine how much your clients' experience of the firm would improve if you were to conclude each case with a completion meeting. Not a quick, patronizing handshake with a junior associate, but a quality meeting with a senior partner of the firm who says, "We are committed to your satisfaction. How did we do? What could we have done better?"

Better yet, show your clients what they mean to you by making a symbolic gesture. For example, during a golf game, a Texas lawyer introduced a client to a large real estate developer. The two men ended up doing business when the client was later contracted to build a huge shopping center. When the deal closed and the papers were signed, the lawyer took his client aside and presented him with a golf ball imprinted with both the client's and the developer's names, courtesy of the law firm. Corny, you might say. Perhaps, but ten years later, the client still has that golf ball sitting on his desk and the lawyer still gets all of his business.

A true symbolic gesture is more than a clever expression. It demonstrates that you took the time to think about the relationship with your client and made it both significant and interesting. Compare this gesture with the all-too-ordinary imprinted pen or calendar sent out to clients once a year.

Effective marketing creates a quality point of contact that demonstrates your commitment to your client. It elicits respect and trust. It acknowledges the importance of the client relationship. And, if done successfully, it will create a lasting and invaluable bond with your firm.

This approach is magnitudes more powerful than coming up with the catchiest jingle or the most sophisticated ad campaign.

A client who is emotionally touched by a relationship will tell everyone about your firm. In terms of generating more business, this kind of marketing is worth ten times the value of a great TV commercial. In terms of personal satisfaction and quality of life—for your clients, your firm and yourself—it's priceless.

Positive Experiences

Understanding "value" requires understanding different types of emotional responses resulting from experiencing different levels of service. Figure 2.3 lists some of the major emotions psychologists associate with positive service experiences.

For every point of contact, it is important to identify the specific emotion elicited from the interaction that made it a *positive* experience.

FIGURE 2.3: Positive service experiences can elicit these positive emotions.

Clients are said to have a positive service experience when they are made to feel:

important	satisfied	calm
valued	pleased	trusted
inspired	comforted	informed
appreciated	protected	cared about
listened to	secure	accepted
understood	confident	respected
pampered	independent	recognized
relaxed	strong	admired

Although these qualities are subjective in nature and cannot be evoked in every client every time, there are some tangible ways to consistently produce positive experiences for your client. The key is to recognize how important it is to generate these types of feelings—then it's astonishing how many opportunities will arise.

One way of making clients feel more secure and confident about their legal predicament is to become a resource of helpful information— especially if what you offer goes beyond legal considerations and is both practical and immediately useful to your client.

Willy Little, a partner in a small Los Angeles firm, described his special brand of value-based service like this:

If we have a client in the midst of a divorce, they often need to find alternative living quarters. They need leases to be reviewed and names of reputable services that can help them with the mundane, but often exhausting, task of relocation.

We're a family law firm. But we are committed to providing our clients with the best service possible. So we do our best to become a resource for our clients—not just in our legal capacity, but in a much broader sense, assisting clients in dealing with the many aspects of divorce. We become a client information hub—an information resource. Clients really appreciate this and, when they need legal help again, they know where to turn.

Sometimes providing superior value to clients means expanding the focus of the legal services a firm offers. Cecilia Smithers, a partner in a midsize litigation firm, remembers the rationale behind a change at her own firm that expanded the firm's zone of contact:

While our firm was litigation-intensive, we felt there were many times it served our clients' interests to consider alternative dispute resolution. To do this effectively, we needed to focus on counseling our clients, which meant making the effort to get to know them and, with some work, earn their trust. We worked with clients to consider alternative points of view whenever possible, which often led to helping them clarify their objectives and think about their situations in new ways.

There can be little doubt that the clients of these firms experienced the service being provided to them in emotionally reassuring ways. Research shows that *experiential marketing*—marketing that addresses a client's needs—is far more effective than the coercion, persuasion and propaganda on which many marketing campaigns are founded.

The Emotional Side

Providing a renowned level of service to clients requires paying attention and being sensitive to the emotional side of legal trouble.

Lawyers who pay attention to clients' subjective experiences are able to expand the scope of legal and practical options available to their clients, which can result in the lawyers becoming better problem solvers.

Old marketing models were based on a number of false assumptions about what influences people's decisions. Now that we know more about how the mind works, we have a unique opportunity to apply this knowledge to the goal of meeting our clients' real needs as opposed to the needs we merely assume they have.

In our legal training, we are taught the paramount importance of *words* and *logic*. Even in the emotional setting of trial, most skilled attorneys—while highly attuned to the emotional reactions of juries—ultimately almost always rely on the persuasive power of logic, words and reason to win their cases.

Today, neuroscience is providing important insights into the ways people interpret information and the degree to which "thinking" is used to influence our decisions. Lawyers' emphasis on words is based largely on the false assumption that most of our thinking takes place in our conscious minds. In fact, recent brain science research reveals that just the opposite is true: As much as 95 percent of our thinking actually takes place at the subconscious level.

Our memories, associations and emotions occur just below the surface of our awareness. In response to stimuli, our minds go busily to work at a staggering speed, networking, sharing, distributing, connecting, shuffling and reshuffling memories, images and thoughts before the first words of reaction ever leave our lips. Ironically, the words we speak are literally an afterthought.

How can this knowledge be applied to the way we communicate and deal with our clients? We would like to assume that clients, for the most part, make decisions deliberately and rationally. That is, that they consciously contemplate the relative merits of a choice, assign a value to each criterion and then convert this information into what we call a judgment. We'd certainly like to assume that's how we make decisions ourselves! But the fact is, most decisions are made at the intuitive, emotional level.

Whether responding to an argument in the courtroom or to a firm's marketing campaign, even the most intelligent people process their decisions below the surface of their conscious mind. In reality, words and logic have more to do with *justifying* a decision than forming the basis of one.

Consider how clients choose law firms. They may think they were led by logic—going with "a big firm" or choosing on the basis of a lawyer's "professional demeanor," but they are actually using their intuition to make what *appears* to be a highly objective decision.

When attorneys learn to think emotionally, they will find new ways to communicate with their clients at the decision-making level. Therefore, providing a renowned level of service to clients means expanding the quality of personal attention given to the emotional side of problem solving. Lawyers who pay attention to clients' subjective experiences are able to offer a wide scope of practical and legal options for their clients to consider.

"We see the same problems over and over again," a partner in a small Cleveland practice explained. "When we know our clients are going through a painful time in their life, our job is often to help them connect the dots at a personal level. This requires us to think emotionally—to become more empathetic—so that we can get inside the minds of our clients. But the truth is, even in the context of law, a client's decision process is driven more strongly by emotion than by any other single factor."

Emotion is a stronger influence on the decision-making process, but words are not even a close second, although it's a common assumption that we think in words.

While words play a central role in communicating thoughts, we rarely use them to think. Using words is just too slow, and language does not contain enough bandwidth to accommodate the complexity of our thinking processes. Feelings can be both instantaneous and complex in ways that words cannot be.

The law firm that recognizes the important role emotions play in its clients' decision-making process and adjusts its service accordingly will find new opportunities to provide clients with increasingly higher levels of service.

Knowledge Sharing

Professional service marketing is both knowledge intensive and relationship intensive. For law firms in particular, knowledge-sharing and relationship building are two essential elements of providing quality legal counsel, and they need to work together. Developing client relationships comes from sharing knowledge in ways that build confidence and trust.

Unfortunately, many lawyers are reluctant to share their knowledge with clients. Some would rather create a shroud of mystery around their work, forcing clients to view them as indispensable—an especially effective technique for a lawyer who has already been successful in solving a prior legal problem for a client. However, this approach almost always results in clients feeling insecure and vulnerable, and it does not lead to the type of trust or loyalty that, in the long run, makes clients return.

Marketing is an empathetic process. It requires that lawyers step back and become observers in the lawyer-client relationship. In doing so, we must detach ourselves from our own views and old ways of thinking. For most of us, this requires a shift in perspective.

Neuroscientists tell us that our minds thrive on exploring new ways of thinking—seeing relationships between things we previously thought were unrelated and finding commonality between different disciplines such as language and the arts or science and philosophy.

The same can be said of the kind of shift in thinking required to connect emotions with marketing and marketing with identity. These new combinations are powerful and effective, but part of the challenge in using them is to first get our minds around them.

The entire range of our thinking, the depth of our very perception, is said to shift when we challenge ourselves to understand the totality of something rather than just our narrow part of it.

Thinking is our forte as lawyers. But true mental strength depends on our willingness to understand different types of thinking—on being able to shift and widen our perspectives and consider new approaches to problem solving.

Challenging our minds means breaking through the linear and narrow confines of our own categorical logic. We need to look beyond the world of opposites—things that are either true or false but never both. In short, we need to stop and take a fresh look at what we do and why we do it. If we hope to provide the kind of high-level service that will set us apart from our competition and create a new magnitude of client satisfaction, we need to see clients' needs in ways we haven't seen before.

This, of course, requires that we develop new ways of thinking. It means leaving our mental comfort zone—not a pleasant proposition for lawyers who have spent years learning how to think in that zone. Yet leaving it is essential if we are committed to the full range of the marketing process.

Service Based on Character

Action that comes from one's character is perceived as authentic and therefore predictable. Ideally, clients will come to know their lawyers as people who can be counted on under almost any circumstances. Lawyers who can be counted on to be responsible, attentive, caring, sensible, honest, hardworking and trustworthy will attract new clients and keep existing ones.

Developing a law firm based on these types of inspired values is what drives firm growth and fosters prosperity. However, character cannot be imposed from the outside. It must originate from the core of the firm's leadership and grow outward. That's why relationship building is so important to our work.

Many law firms balk at investing in education and personal development. Mentoring is too often limited to developing technical skills such as research and drafting. Developing lawyers' communication and character-building skills has been devalued, and this reflects the degree of resignation and cynicism existing in our profession today. Ironically, the same firms that don't value personal development wonder why they're experiencing a staggering drop in client satisfaction.

The Trust Factor

Do clients see you as someone they trust? As someone who is honest with them and acts with integrity? Are you seen as someone who truly cares about their welfare?

What we *do* for our clients reveals not only our immediate *intentions*, but also our character.

Clients measure our service first and foremost—but not completely—by our actions. If our actions are perceived to arise naturally from our character, then we are perceived as sincere and trustworthy. If not, which all too often is the case, we can appear calculating and manipulative.

Clients trust their lawyers if they believe in the truth of the lawyers' character. For lawyers to learn to serve from their character takes time, effort and a commitment to individual development. Despite popular opinion, character *can* be developed and learned, especially if it is enforced by the firm's culture and leadership. Thus, the term *character building*.

For most firms, however, developing communication skills in their lawyers is simply not a priority. In fact, some firms believe that it's not necessary if they simply hire quality people.

"When we recruit, we look for young people who have a strong sense of purpose," said a partner at an East Coast firm. "To our firm, this means maturity, manners and common sense. Sure, we want the brightest minds, but we refuse to compromise on character. We won't give an offer unless we believe in our gut that person can truly grow into being a partner."

Lawyers who are truly valued by their clients develop client relationships that grow into alliances. At the other end of the spectrum are lawyers who view their job as opening and closing files. They exist in a virtual dead zone— a place where the personal side of the client's experience is not relevant, the client having been reduced to just another "fact" in a set of issues belonging to a file making up a unit of revenue.

Somewhere along the line, these lawyers have come to believe that as long as there is sufficient revenue flow, fixing and changing the exterior problems (applying the hammer) will be sufficient to keep declining service in check. In the meantime, the partners keep partnering and hope that no one notices that they don't have a clue about where the firm is going or how it will end up.

Without a moral center, there can be no group intention or direction. Instead, there is just the "organization" operating on cruise control, applying superficial fixes to problematic contact points where service and performance have fallen to unacceptable levels.

Accountability

Consider what it means to be accountable to your clients. When clients put their trust in you, what does that mean specifically—to you and to your firm?

Accountability can be viewed as the process by which a firm either succeeds or fails to make and keep its promises. What types of promises? The types that come from the firm's inspired values—those that originate from the moral center of the firm—the "V" spot.

One partner had a very clear sense of what his firm promises: "Our clients count on us to be dependable, honest and totally committed to their interests all the time, every time."

Take the time to identify just three character traits that clients can count on your firm to deliver. As an experiment, list these traits on paper and ask a few other people at your firm to come up with their own list. You'll be surprised at how the responses will vary from person to person.

Consider this: If a firm can't agree on what its clients should expect, chances are, neither can its clients. This is exactly why a firm must define for itself what it means to be in the service of its clients. Only with a clear understanding of its inspired values can a firm hope to provide clients with a consistent experience of exceptional service that they will long remember.

Becoming Client-Centric

A lawyer was killed crossing the street. When he arrived at the Gates of Heaven, God welcomed him warmly.

"You're happy to see me?" asked the lawyer hesitantly. "Well, 'happy' may be pushing it," said God, "But we certainly are pleased—you know, we get so few lawyers up here that we always treat it like a special occasion when one arrives. But most importantly, we want to make sure you'll be happy in heaven. After all, we wouldn't want you to 'rush to judgment.'" God laughed and asked, "Hey, isn't that a legal phrase?"

God told the lawyer he could spend one full day in Hell and one full day in Heaven so he could experience both. He said the lawyer would then be free to decide where to spend eternity.

God escorted the lawyer to the elevator.

He pushed the basement button and told the lawyer to keep an open mind.

The elevator took the lawyer down—all the way down— and when the doors opened, he saw a beautiful golf course. All his old friends were there in fine suits, cheering for him, slapping him on the back and telling stories. He was then introduced to the Devil, who seemed like a really nice guy. Everyone shared jokes, drank fine wine and ate sushi.

After enjoying a wonderful dessert, it was time for the lawyer to leave Hell and head up to Heaven. His day in Heaven was also nice. He played the harp, floated on clouds and sang beautiful songs. When the lawyer's day in Heaven was over, God said it was time for him to choose.

The lawyer said, "I never thought I would say this, but I think I'll have to choose Hell."

Down went the lawyer in the elevator. When the door opened, he saw a dark wasteland, covered in garbage and smelling revolting. His friends were dressed in rags and were bone-thin. Misery was everywhere.

"I don't understand," the lawyer said to the smiling Devil. "Yesterday, this was a beautiful golf course with dancing and cheer. What happened?"

The Devil put his arm around the lawyer and said, "That's because yesterday you were a prospect, but today you're a client!"

When I first heard this joke, my response was probably like yours— amusement. Then I began to wonder whether there might be some truth in the tale. I began to experience a queasy feeling in the pit of my stomach as I wondered how clients might react after being wined and dined by a firm only to be disappointed with the firm's service soon after they become clients.

While such disappointment might not happen as abruptly as an elevator door opening on the pits of Hell, it can happen gradually if a firm's service deteriorates and the client begins to feel taken for granted.

Sometimes clients are not only taken for granted, but they may also be shown disrespect without a law firm's being aware of it.

We must remember that going to a lawyer often involves taking a risk. One's personal life and all the troubles that go along with it are suddenly in the hands of strangers. Clients need to be convinced that they will be respected and receive serious attention.

Listen to the vulnerability in this client's story:

My marriage was coming to an end. I was in a bitter divorce and I was emotionally exhausted. My lawyer had set up a last-minute meeting at his office between the parties to see if we could settle before trial. My spouse and her lawyer joined me and my lawyer in a conference room.

The atmosphere was uncomfortable. I remember how hard my heart was beating as the custody of our two children was discussed. My lawyer made some good points on my behalf. There was a brief lull in the conversation and, out of nowhere, my lawyer asked my wife's lawyer if he was going to the annual family law conference that month. They talked a while about hotels and kidded about which ones were known to have the larger roaches. They had a few laughs, and as they made their way back to the matters at hand, my spouse and I just looked at each other, dumfounded.

There, on that conference table, amid the papers and boxes, were our whole lives and the lives of our children. I thought how utterly unprofessional it was for our lawyers to talk about continuing education as if we weren't even there. I never told my lawyer how I felt about that incident. I'm not even sure he would know what I was talking about, but I was deeply offended.

It's easy to forget that lawyers trade in matters of great importance to their clients' lives. Perhaps because of this, we seek moments of relief by stepping outside our formal roles to seek some levity or engage in less emotionally charged matters—maybe it's a way of resting our minds so that we can better focus when we return to the serious matters at hand. But when we do this in the presence of our clients, we do it at risk of offending them. The clients must know that our time with them is precious and is focused on them and their issues. They must feel, at least for the time we are with them, that they are our only clients. It is the highly personal nature of legal trouble that accounts for clients' heightened sensitivity. This is true whether it's corporate law or consumer law.

Fulfilling Clients' Emotional Needs

Great marketing begins with honest reflection—a willingness to examine the collective identity of the firm and its purpose. Firms must see themselves as they are today and then carefully choose what they will be tomorrow. If they do this in the specific context of fulfilling their clients' emotional needs, they may be able to reach the absolute zenith in the art of marketing.

Ironically, once your firm attains this level, promotion will no longer feel or sound like promotion. It will feel and sound like your firm. At this point, saying who you are and what you offer will be as natural as saying your name. It will be evident in the way you go about your business, the criteria you use to hire new people, and the way you treat your clients and those considering becoming clients. It is communication in its purest form.

Marketing Gone Wrong

If providing clients with a positive experience with your firm is the equivalent of excellent marketing, then providing clients with a negative experience is the equivalent of running a negative ad, because when clients choose to take their business elsewhere, they often make it their mission in life to tell the world why.

Unfortunately, clients may also take their business elsewhere when marketing is not done at all or is done poorly—when there is a palpable inconsistency between what a firm *says* it stands for and what it *does*. There is no hiding such an inconsistency, and nothing breeds as much distrust and alienation as not being who you say you are. Rather than look in the mirror, firms tend to ignore this issue. In desperation, and possibly in ignorance, firms begin to engage in promotional tactics that are either unnecessary or manipulative.

Many marketers choose to exploit the emotional dimension of service marketing. While addressing the emotional component makes sense, the wrong kind of campaign can actually drive clients away.

Campaigns that play on emotional triggers have dominated the legal landscape in recent years. They are frequently backed by huge advertising budgets, and they center around campaigns that are designed to appeal to fear, greed or ego, playing to clients' vulnerabilities. Each type of campaign is emotionally driven and problematic in its own way. Campaigns focusing on an appeal to fear disempower clients; an appeal to greed obsesses them; and an appeal to ego creates in them a false sense of power. Rarely, if ever, are these approaches effective in the long run—they appear to work in the beginning, but quickly lose steam and crash.

Emotional Vulnerability

Campaigns that target negative emotions focus on specific feelings that dominate people who are experiencing certain types of legal trouble. This focus can be seen in all forms of communication aimed at potential clients and can be extraordinarily subtle. Fear and greed are powerful motivating forces. Fear takes all shapes and forms. People fear losing what they already have. Some even fear losing what they *don't* have, such as an inheritance or a job opportunity.

It's not that firms deliberately exploit their clients' emotions. On the contrary, most firms believe that the single most important role of lawyers is to protect and promote their clients' interests. But an ad campaign can inadvertently create a negative reaction by using marketing that concentrates on emotional manipulation.

Fear Is Multidimensional

Fear takes many forms. People in legal trouble are especially vulnerable to fear because they are anticipating some type of loss. It could be a loss of income, job opportunity, spouse, home, business, reputation or health— even a loss of freedom.

The loss that comes from most legal trouble is usually, at least to some extent, life changing. So it is not only the *fear* of loss that makes people feel so vulnerable, it's also not knowing the *consequences* that can result from their loss.

In fact, it is well established that fear of the unknown is high on the list of what worries people. Not knowing what will happen causes people to search out answers from people who do; we call these people professionals. People in legal trouble justifiably want information, and they want it now. They want to know: How bad is it? How bad can it get? What do I need to know? What should I expect? What are my options? What does your experience tell you I should do?

Fear-Based Campaigns

Fear-based campaigns are not always the work of small firms. Nor is the audience made up only of consumers. Such campaigns are used at very high levels and with very sophisticated clients.

One prominent national law firm (now bankrupt) spent tens of millions of dollars on a national television campaign directed at corporate America. The central message was: *Retain our firm when the future of your business depends on it.*

At first glance, this campaign seemed fairly benign. Yet the message was actually very powerful. Implicit in it was the submessage *If you don't use our firm, you may not have a future.*

Not having a "future" implies being rendered nonexistent. That's advertising talk for saying you're dead. No other fear is as powerful, motivating or pervasive—and Madison Avenue knows it.

Unquestionably fear messages motivate clients, but at what expense? Lawyers have also used television and telephone books to send their messages. Recognize any of the taglines in Figure 3.1? Fear of loss is frequently central to these types of campaigns. These ads use the vulnerability of clients to try to increase their business.

FIGURE 3.1: Fear-Based Advertising Messages

ADVERTISING MESSAGE	INFERENCE OF VULNERABILITY
Don't Lose Your Rights!	I don't know any better!
Stop the Creditors!	I have no control over my life!
Denied Coverage?	I'm being taken advantage of!
Save Your Home!	I'll have no place to go!
Don't Settle for Less!	I should know better!
Get Protection Now!	Time is against me!
Stop Wage Garnishment!	They're coming to get me!
Stop Harassment!	I'm being victimized!
Don't Risk a Wrong Decision!	I'm not smart enough to make choices!
Don't Risk Your Assets!	I'm not responsible!
Don't Be Railroaded!	I'm stupid and people take advantage of me!

Greed-Based Campaigns

Greed is actually a form of fear—a fear that creates the belief that there is not enough and will never be enough to feel truly satisfied and complete. In this sense, greed may also be viewed as a type of vulnerability.

Fear is a primordial emotion derived from our instinctive ability to perceive and respond to danger. The fight-or-flight instinct has been hardwired into our minds. *Greed*, on the other hand, is not entirely instinctual. It's been said that greed is one of those miserable forms of ignorance that keeps us from knowing our potential.

Some lawyers lure clients with promises of large financial gain to play to clients' greed. While most lawyers stay within ethical bounds, some cross the line without even being aware of it. This is especially true in the area of personal injury.

While it has been argued that "fighting language" used in advertising is intended to demonstrate a lawyer's zeal and unfettered advocacy style, it appears to the general public as self-serving rhetoric. Small type at the bottom of such lawyers' ads disclaiming any implicit promise of specific results or recovery does not solve the problem.

Most professionals agree that advertising intended to appeal to a client's greed is manipulative and insulting. It can unwittingly inflate a client's expectations and erode a lawyer's credibility. And in the end it does little to advance the image of the profession.

Appealing to Ego: Romancing the Client

Traditionally, larger firms have relied on entertaining clients in hopes of getting more business. Unfortunately, lawyers more interested in strutting their legal feathers than listening to their clients can squander these valuable opportunities to learn about clients' specific needs.

Breaking bread with a prospective client has been the hallmark of rainmaking. And as any skilled rainmaker will tell you, it must be done masterfully.

Here is how one jaded rainmaker described the courting ritual:

> *First, it requires the right restaurant—preferably one that shows a flair for glamour. At the table, a drink before dinner is customary, followed by a few war stories that demonstrate our firm's courage and our relentless dedication to our clients. Then it's time to drop a few names. We handle the very best clients. Ideally, the alcohol has entered the client's bloodstream before I unleash a few of my better jokes.*
>
> *The good humor is intended to lighten the mood and demon-*

strate wit, after which it's time for a few well rehearsed ques-tions aimed specifically at the client's legal matter. Bang! Bang! The client is taken totally by surprise. He fumbles his words. The moment becomes awkward. I listen intently. I nod with understanding—and, like the patient lad I am, I wait for the client to tell me a bit about his problems. And at just the right moment, I steer the conversation back to our firm and how we can help him out of that horrible mess he got himself into.

When the check comes, I always let it sit for a few moments. This shows patience. Then I pull out the firm's Gold Card and pay for the meal. This shows generosity. If the restaurant per-mits, I might offer the client a cigar—a way of implicitly ac-knowledging our bond. And of course, the deal sealer, a small envelope bearing front-row tickets to the big game.

All of this, of course, is window dressing. Clients may engage in the courting process, but inside they frequently distrust it. They see it as con-descending, manipulative and self-serving. They don't believe the lawyer's interest in them is sincere. They are more inclined to believe he views them as just another stream of billable hours.

Today, romancing of the kind described above is actually unnecessary. It's as stale and unproductive as yesterday's three-martini lunch. What cli-ents really want is to be listened to and respected.

Clients know when they are being romanced, and it can backfire in big ways. One partner shared this unfortunate experience that happened while courting a rather large insurance company.

It was the eighties, and we were looking for more business from this one insurance company. We found out that one of their top claims people loved to go bird-shooting—doves to be exact—so we arranged a holiday hunting trip and invited some of the claims people as the firm's guests.

It was early morning and we were sitting in a field of mud just waiting. When we heard the sudden flurry of the birds, one of our guns accidentally discharged. Some of the pellets ended up in the backside of one of the claims adjusters. Luckily, the pellets dispersed well and he was not seriously hurt. The trip ended rather abruptly. When the president of the company found out about the incident, he was livid and reprimanded his people for accepting our invitation. We never did see another file from them.

Focusing on Finding Solutions

Fear-based campaigns make clients feel vulnerable and exploited. It's rare that clients are benefited by having their fears and worries reinforced or amplified. What clients really want is a lawyer who will help them make sense of their problem and figure out how to solve it. To do this well, lawyers must hone their interpersonal communication skills.

Clients are anxious during legal consultations. In an effort to avoid looking uninformed, lawyers sometimes rush into the legal issues, perhaps offering a provocative legal theory. In doing so, they miss an opportunity to understand the client, when what the client really wants is for them to listen.

Unless the client really opens up and unless the lawyer really takes the time to understand, the lawyer will not truly and fully know how to advise the client. Knowing the law is great, but clients really want to know how it pertains to them and how it will specifically affect their lives—which requires that the lawyer understand what's important to them. And often, clients won't tell the lawyer until they trust him.

Legal problems do not exist in a vacuum. They are multidimensional and affect many aspects of a client's life. The entirety of the client's life situation must be considered and factored into our work if we are to be true problem solvers—if we are to provide a higher quality of service. A lawyer who is committed to the client cannot ignore the totality of this challenge.

Marketing is a fluid process. It is often a product of people's expectations of your firm, and, in particular, exactly what your firm can be counted on to do—not just for its clients, but for everyone who comes into contact with it, from the office supply salesman, to the partners, to the new associates. Every part of the firm—the way it looks, how people work together and its work product—becomes part of the same message.

If the message is given properly, the firm will develop a persona—a way of being that is unique. Different media communicate in different ways and have their own strengths and weaknesses, but together they can form a unified message. Whether communication is visual, auditory, sensory or simply a producer of "good vibes," all of it contributes to the firm's message.

Context Marketing™

Providing *service* means nothing without understanding *context*. Context is the full dimension of the life events and surrounding circumstances that gave rise to a client's need to see a lawyer in the first place. Understanding the context of a client's problem requires a broad understanding of clients and their circumstances as well as a recognition of the importance of both the subjective and objective side of any client problem.

> Context Marketing *is a process in which* service *is defined and implemented within the* context *of the specific needs and desires of the client.*

Lawyers are most useful when they help clients to uncover the full scope of their interests. Sometimes this requires that lawyers assist clients in separating the facts and logic of a problem from its emotional side.

Proactively helping clients to discover the full range of their options can help them to identify possible solutions they would not previously have considered.

For those who think that lawyers are entering the domain of psychologists and family counselors by giving this kind of emotional attention, consider this: By encouraging the client to work with you in thinking proactively and creatively, opportunities not visible before can lead to new pathways of problem solving. More often than not, this type of thinking will help clients find resolution to both their legal and nonlegal troubles.

Defining marketing in this way requires us to first acknowledge the client's role in the relationship. As obvious as this first step might seem, most firms overlook it.

Life Context

Figure 3.2 illustrates the depth of context-based marketing. Clients come to a lawyer for legal help, but many other concerns appear just as significant as the legal ones—concerns that have very real and emotional consequences that often cannot be solved with a solely "legal" solution.

FIGURE 3.2: Legal Concerns vs. Life Context Concerns

LEGAL CONCERNS	LIFE CONTEXT CONCERNS
What if I get a divorce?	What will my children think?
Am I entitled to permanent disability?	How will I educate my children?
Can my company terminate my employment?	Where do I go to find a job?
What if our product was defective?	How will the board react?
What if the partnership dissolves?	What will my competition think?
What if I am accused of malpractice?	Will it ruin my reputation?
What if I go bankrupt?	Will my new employer find out?
What if a competitor steals our client?	Will other clients lose confidence?
What if we hire our competitor's top employee?	Will it show weakness?
What if the contract is one-sided?	Will they question my integrity?
What if our advertising wasn't accurate?	Will we lose our customer confidence?
What if we go through probate?	Will I have to deal with my brother?
What if I was sexually harassed?	Will I be labeled a troublemaker?
What if I lose my driver's license?	Will I lose my business?

Lawyers often ignore their clients' life concerns by focusing solely on their legal questions. When this happens, lawyers miss a golden opportunity to build clients' confidence and trust in the firm. Clients don't expect us to fix all their problems, but they *do* want us to at least acknowledge their pain and understand their major concerns.

Becoming Client-Centric

Context Marketing requires that we focus on clients' experiences first and foremost. The range of their concerns is illustrated in Figure 3.3.

The outside circle represents the functional aspects of the legal matter for which the client has sought counsel. Within this ring we find such tasks as drafting and preparing documents, rendering legal advice and appearing in court.

FIGURE 3.3: The Client-Centric Consumer Model

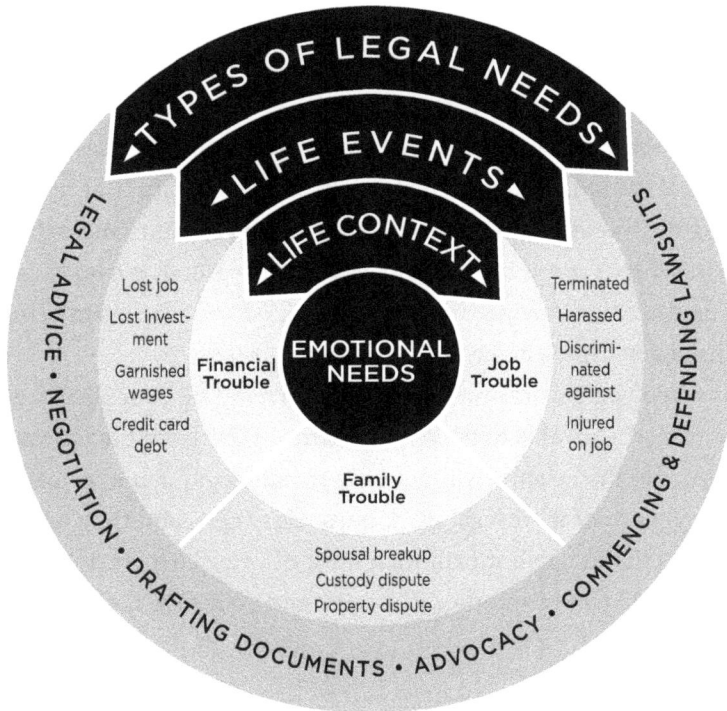

For example, if the reason the client is seeking counsel is a divorce, most lawyers will see their scope of responsibility as falling within the limited confines of the outer ring—the legal task presented—to the exclusion of most other client concerns. However, by limiting the scope in this way, lawyers limit their opportunities to provide a higher level of service.

The client may need to relocate and find new housing quickly. Sufficient storage might be an issue. A counselor or psychologist may be needed. For many clients, legal issues represent the onset of a profound change in their lives and often come with emotional upheaval.

Rarely, however, will lawyers offer insight, encouragement or guidance into what they consider the *practical and mundane* concerns that are secondary to the legal issue at hand. They ignore the client's life context, and in doing so, they lose a valuable opportunity to serve their client at a deeper, more personal level.

If we are to define what excellent service means, a good starting point is to examine how our clients perceive the firm and its services—specifically, what it is your clients expect from you and your firm. This is the first step in becoming client-centric.

The objective and subjective sides to service are meaningless unless we understand the underlying context in which they operate. This means first knowing the full dimension of the life events and circumstances that gave rise to the client's specific needs and wants. And second, it requires understanding the emotional implications associated with the client's changed circumstances. This is being client-centric at its best.

It is when you become masterful at understanding your clients' expectations that you are able to go *beyond* them—to perform the unexpected! When you do this, clients will not only remain loyal, but also make sure that every piece of their legal work goes your way—and they will spend more time talking up your firm than most of your partners do! Combine this with intelligent promotion strategies, and your firm has the power to be unstoppable.

Measuring Perceived Value

When quality of service meets clients' expectations, the service is said to have value—but how much?

Value is highest when performance exceeds expectations. It's the qualitative difference between being treated in an ordinary way and being treated in a *special* way.

At the *minimum*, clients expect to receive a value commensurate with the fee paid. If the quality of service falls substantially short of that expectation, clients are not only disappointed, but they can also feel cheated.

Ultimately, clients determine value, both at a subjective level and at an objective level. However, the emotional nature of legal trouble is such that it often overshadows many of their other concerns. Understanding this is fundamental to meeting and exceeding your clients' expectations. It is the key to the way clients measure value and to building a loyal client base.

Loyal Clients/Lost Clients

A client determines value at multiple levels. While most lawyers believe that competently and professionally representing their clients' objective legal interests will alone create the loyalty they seek from clients, this is most often not the case.

From the clients' perspective, it is *assumed* that you are professionally competent to handle their matter. After all, if the state issued you a license, you must be competent. What clients don't know is whether you genuinely care about their welfare and whether you will take the time to understand their unique situation—the life context behind their legal trouble. Again, it is in the subjective realm that value is ultimately determined. Figure 3.4 (see next page) shows the different levels of service perceived by clients.

FIGURE 3.4: Three levels of service perceived by clients

I **SUBSTANDARD SERVICE**	II **ACCEPTABLE SERVICE**	III **EXCELLENT SERVICE**
Objective needs not met	Objective needs met	Objective needs met
Subjective needs not met	Subjective needs not met	Subjective needs met
Life context unknown	Life context known	Life context addressed
Expectations not met	Expectations met	Expectations surpassed
Perceived value low	Perceived value ordinary	Perceived value excellent
Client disappointed	Client unmoved	Client inspired
Result: lost client	**Result: retained client**	**Result: loyal client**

Practical Concerns

How does a firm take on the challenge of knowing a client? One not-soobvious step is to be realistic about the scope of the firm's practice, specifically the number of practice areas the firm intends to master.

Providing service in multiple practice areas can be problematic. This is especially true in small general-practice firms that accept cases outside of their field of expertise. It has been said that it is better to be *something to someone* than *everything to everyone*. Trying to be everything to everyone has been the curse of the solo practice. Not only is the learning curve high, but doing this is also usually time intensive. Recent surveys have shown a sharp decline in these types of practices.

Trying to be everything to everyone is not as big a problem in larger firms. Such firms have the resources to develop autonomous practice groups. Lawyers within these groups can serve clients well within their area of expertise, and they also understand clients' life contexts. If clients need expertise not serviced by a practice group, they can be introduced to another group within the firm. This is a marked advantage of such highly resourced firms. However, these firms don't always recognize their advantage and therefore don't fully exploit it.

Know Your Clients' Dreams

Every client has different needs. The goal is to understand each client from his or her own perspective. For business clients, it means spending time learning as much as possible about their business, history, competition and challenges. Being client-centric means having a sincere interest in your clients' challenges and goals as well as their problems.

Oddly enough, most lawyers find inquiring about clients' needs quite unsettling. Some express concern that delving into matters of the heart can get messy; it can upset and offend, and may even result in losing the client.

In truth, most lawyers just find it awkward and say that it makes *them* feel vulnerable. Most would rather not have their clients view them as sensitive and kind, but rather as powerful and stoic. However, the fact is that clients usually prefer lawyers that are sensitive and kind. With sensitivity comes a willingness to know more about the client. It is a form of knowledge building—and with knowledge comes power.

In the world of commerce, successful corporations spend tens of millions of dollars every year just to find out what their customers think and feel about them. Indeed, in the service business, knowledge *is* power.

Serving Businesses

Knowing more about your clients makes you more valuable to them. Business clients are no exception.

Every client file should contain a detailed client summary—not just notes on the initial client meeting, but a detailed summary that articulates the client's current situation, the context within which the legal concern arose and a concise statement of the client's expectations.

The summary should include the names of the client's key people, including their executive secretaries and support staff. If possible, it should contain the client's business preferences such as whether they prefer early or late meetings and whether they prefer meeting at your office or theirs.

The goal is to discover your client's individual preferences.

Make sure that every member of your team has read the client's summary. Thereafter, make sure that every new partner, lawyer, secretary and staff member who works on the file—as a matter of firm policy—reads and knows the essential components of the summary.

Accumulate this information from your clients—and then figure out specific ways to deliver the services they desire.

One way of building trust is to get to know a client's long-range plans—where they see themselves three to five years from now. As clients tell you about their plans, try to picture the future scenario in your mind and help clients to fill in the details. By learning your clients' visions, you are sharing and participating in their creative process. This is a tremendous way to bond with your clients, and it will help you to better anticipate their future needs.

Ask clients questions like "How do you see building out your sales department in the next three years? Will that be done through your communications division? I see where you're going. How do you think the competition will respond? I can see how that will require ramping up your various teams. Tell me how you envision your executive team."

One way to know your clients better is to ask better questions—lots of them. Learning about their particular business context and their concerns will often give you the unexpected benefit of learning more about their legal needs, and it can also reveal their emotional connection to their problems. Every client, of course, is different. Not all clients will share their deep concerns and feelings. But don't think this means they're not experiencing them. How much you learn about them will depend on how much they trust you—and trust is something that is earned slowly and usually only after clients believe your intentions are sincere.

If you really get to know your clients, you can literally define what "excellent service" means to them. Imagine having *this* in your client summary!

With business clients, there can be even more opportunities to serve well, and the need to be client-centric is just as important. One way to serve is by thinking preventively—by paying attention to clients' needs before legal problems arise.

Max Aloette, a commercial lawyer in Houston, shared this story:

> *We represent healthcare providers in contract disputes. A few years ago, I was visiting one of our smaller hospital clients when I learned that one of the main risk managers had been assigned the responsibility of HIPAA compliance. I knew who she was, so I stopped by to see how she was doing. Not long into the conversation it became clear that she felt overwhelmed in this new area.*
>
> *When I got back to my office, I made a call to another client who was a very experienced compliance officer. I explained the situation to him and asked if he would have lunch with me and the small-hospital manager and help her to become more familiar with HIPAA compliance. The lunch was very productive. A year later, there was a staff change at the hospital, and the small-hospital manager moved up to senior risk manager. It wasn't long before we started being assigned more work from that hospital.*

Let's examine the principles of context marketing in relation to this example. Looking at the client's experience with Max's firm, it can be said the client was made to feel valued, protected, cared for, empowered, comforted and understood. She had a very positive experience with the firm, precisely because Max took the time to understand her context—which, in this case, meant being attentive to the subjective concerns that surrounded her need to know more about health compliance rules while not appearing uninformed to her organization.

Max exceeded this client's expectation. What he did wasn't about law and it wasn't about fees. It was about helping a client through the fear of learning a new area. It would have been easy to simply give this client the phone number of the other client and let her initiate contact. Instead, he was sensitive to her feelings, perhaps thinking that she would feel uncomfortable or embarrassed making the call herself. Max went even further out of his way by setting up and attending a lunch to make the personal introduction. He was taking care of the *subjective* needs of his client.

Another very important fact is that Max also chose not to bill his client for the time he spent calling and meeting—instead the time sheet showed "No charge." The positive impact of such a gesture cannot be underestimated. It is what turns satisfied clients into inspired clients.

Remember, your existing clients are your best source of business, so serve them well. Your firm's reputation is quite literally in their hands.

The Big Fee Myth

When pricing a product, it is said that price should reflect a *quid pro quo* for value received. Price, however, communicates much more. It tells us about the assumptions people use in determining value. A higher price normally implies a higher value. Price is said to affect even the experience of using a product.

Studies show that people are actually attracted to higher-priced products because price is seen as predictive of quality. The converse is also true: People expect lower-priced products to be lower in quality than higher-priced ones.

In law, as in most professional services, the issue of price presents a unique challenge on the value spectrum. Compared to the value of a product, which is tangible and feature-driven, the value of service is much more difficult to define. But clients know valuable service when they experience it.

Justifying a premium hourly rate has more to do with the quality of your service than any other single factor, including the prevailing market rate. Clients expect to pay more for superior service. In fact, clients' perceived value of quality counsel is reinforced by a premium hourly rate. Studies have shown that when selecting a service, clients who can afford either a low or a high price are three times as likely to choose the higher price. It is well-known that increasing price will not, in itself, decrease the demand for a service. In fact, the opposite may happen.

Sometimes lawyers put more significance on their fees than on their clients. For most clients, the quality of the service—the level of trust and the degree to which their lawyer is truly committed to them—is more important than the money they spend.

Commercial litigator Bradley Carson, from Phoenix, shared this story:

> *A guy called me from my Rotary Club, upset about a small claims matter. He wanted my help, but I told him retaining me would not be financially feasible. Besides, I was a commercial litigation lawyer, not a small claims adviser. I told him it wouldn't be worth the fees to fight it, but he insisted, saying it was a matter of principle.*
>
> *Sure enough, we got a good result, but his legal fees ended up being more than he recovered. I knew he was going to be angry. I reminded him that I had told him it wouldn't make economic sense to pursue the case. He held his ground and asked me to think about reducing the bill. At first I was upset; I had known this was going to happen.*
>
> *Later that week, after I'd cooled down, I reviewed the bill and noticed that I had billed him for every minute I had spent on the case. I didn't do the customary "no charge" for client phone calls, as was often my practice. The more I thought about it, the more I realized I was billing hard because I didn't like working on the case.*
>
> *When I saw him at the Rotary, I took him aside and told him I wanted to make it right with him. We ended up agreeing to split the bill in half. He took out his checkbook and wrote me a check for $1,500 and we shook hands. I felt relieved but uncomfortable. I couldn't help but wonder if he was sincere*

or just grinding me. What happened next almost floored me.

At the end of the meeting, he stood up and told the group that I had won a big case for him (he didn't mention it was small claims) and that I was a fine lawyer and a fine man. He said that, in light of my great work on his case, from the proceeds he was going to be making a contribution in my name to the club's children's fund. The amount: $1,500— his part of the discounted fee.

After that experience, I never looked at clients in the same way.

Becoming client-centric requires shifting your perspective. In fact, it requires you to view the services you provide from the clients' perspective. In doing so, you will discover what specific objective and subjective needs are important. This knowledge is the foundation from which you will articulate what service actually means relative to your clients' expectations. Then you will know what needs to be done to exceed those expectations.

For some attorneys, this shift to a client-centric perspective is more challenging than they would like to admit. Thinking emotionally—probing into clients' personal lives and exploring their subjective satisfaction—seems disturbingly nebulous. After all, lawyers are paid to *think*, not to *feel*.

What happened to the comfortable, logical, linear thinking we learned in law school? What happened to the need to avoid risk, watch our backs, play it safe—and most of all, never admit to uncertainty and never let them see us sweat?

Lawyers are also taught and trained to be language driven—weaving words into sentences and sentences into arguments, which are then carefully slotted into accepted logical abstractions. But it's intuition that ultimately seems to rule us. No matter how compelling an argument may be, in the context of words and logic, it is what we feel and know internally to be true that guides our decisions and judgments.

It has been said that words and logic are the essential tools of a lawyer's craft. Consequently, lawyers tend to rely more on words than on the emotions they produce.

As wordsmiths, lawyers tend to view words as if they were the actual things words describe, rather than being representative of those things. As a result, lawyers—like other professionals who work with words—tend to overidentify language with reality. This can result in getting lost in our own abstractions as we underestimate the deeply subjective and experiential side of what ultimately is communicated to others. We tend to overlook the visual maze of mental pictures, senses and feelings, which studies now show to be the real moving forces behind our actions and choices.

How often do we craft what we consider to be compelling and cogent legal arguments only to have them fall upon the Court's deaf ears? How often have we heard that judges really base their decisions on what they internally feel is right under the circumstances and then find the legal justification to support these intuitive findings? Consider that our entire jury system is based on near reverence for group intuition—a collective sense of what is true or false, right or wrong.

After years of practice, legal skills are second nature to most attorneys. But the truth is, superior service demands that lawyers take another look at their roles with clients. Lawyers are paid to think, but they must admit that their clients are not buying only their technical knowledge and skill.

Whether or not they know it consciously, clients are buying a special type of *relationship*—one they expect will be based on trust and confidence. Part of marketing, therefore, must come from understanding the lawyer's role as a counselor and not just as a legal technician.

Problem-solving must address the emotional side of clients' needs. Traditionally, this area has been considered outside the accepted domain of a lawyer's role, and adding it to our services requires that we reexamine what it means to be a legal thinker and, in a broader sense, precisely what lawyers are paid to do.

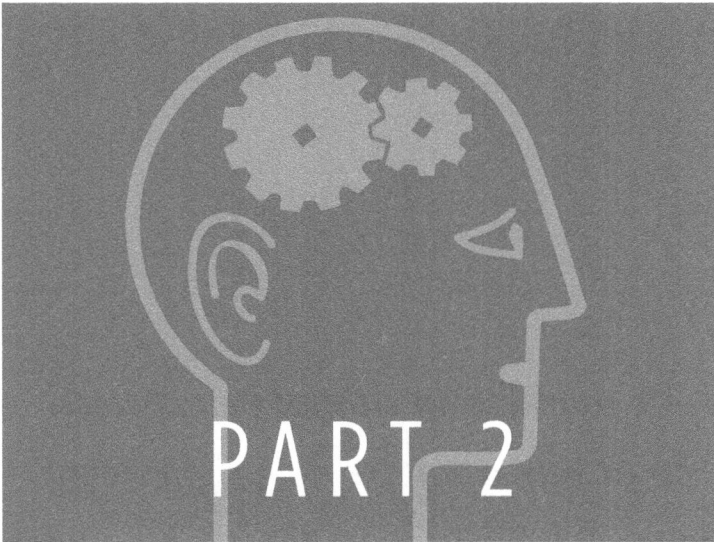

PART 2

Thinking About Thinking

"*A round man cannot be expected to fit into a square hole right away. He must have time to modify his shape.*"

MARK TWAIN

Thinking Like a Lawyer

While most lawyers like to think of themselves as open-minded and objective people, more often than not it is precisely the type of thinking that makes lawyers highly effective at practicing law that can make them ineffective at marketing and managing their firm.

What is it about the legal mind that makes marketing so challenging for lawyers? Part of the answer is that lawyers are easily drawn into linear thinking in their quest toward the right answer—so much so that the need to find the *right answer* becomes the very obstacle to reaching it. One way of understanding this dilemma is to consider that it is not always finding the right answer that is needed, but rather a willingness to find a different perspective in the problem-solving process.

Ironically, when it comes to marketing, it's often the way lawyers *think* about the problem that is the problem.

Thinking Like a Lawyer

As first-year law students we were taught that to become lawyers, we would have to first learn to think like lawyers. Thinking like lawyers required a change in our quality of thinking—in our way of reasoning. It's a daunting premise from which to begin a three-year education.

The process of intellectual transformation from *normal* mind to *lawyer* mind occurs through what law schools refer to as the Socratic method. In fact, it was Socrates who urged us to engage in the process of self examination—in short, to think about how we think.

Memory, while important to success in law school, stands at a distant second when compared to the importance placed on learning how to reason like a lawyer. Law professors like nothing more than ferreting out students who might memorize well but cannot think through issues on their feet. Thinking like a lawyer demands thinking within the confines of inductive and deductive forms of reasoning.

We, as law students, were thrown into this process literally brain-first. We entered a world of rigorous dialogue in which abstractions are formulated and then described—usually leading to the discovery of a general principle or rule, which was then distinguished from others. We learned how to narrow and intensify our focus. And in the Pavlovian spirit, we were rewarded when these tasks were performed well and ridiculed when they were not.

It was a process by which we also learned how to think defensively: We learned how to protect clients (and ourselves) and why we need to proceed slowly, find the traps, measure the risks and never, ever, forget there's always a potential downside lurking behind every set of facts.

How Many Cases?

As students, we soon discovered that there was more work than could be realistically accomplished—unless, of course, we spent almost every waking hour in pursuit of legal knowledge. The competitive nature of the learning process drove us even harder, reinforcing some views and perceptions while diminishing others—all of which would eventually alter the very nature of how we thought. The goal, of course, was for us to become rational, logical thinkers—categorical, linear thinkers—trained to separate that which is reasonable from that which is not and that which is true from that which is false.

It was only a matter of time until the values we learned in law school began to spill over into our personal lives. Unconsciously, we begin to relate to and observe others within the context of our new way of thinking. It began to color our views, opinions and judgments. In the process, we lost some friends and acquired new ones who were more likely to see and understand the world as we did.

In a sense, we began to so identify with our new way of thinking that we unwittingly *became* the thinker—there was no longer a separation between *thinking* that way and *being* that way.

Having learned to think in a new way, we had less tolerance for ambiguity. A new mental structure was forming—a new set of lenses through which to view the structure of human affairs. It was everything we had hoped for—a quantum leap forward; a kind of intellectual transcendence. We had every reason to believe that soon we would be paid to think.

No one doubts the value of a legal education. The sheer mental gymnastics necessary to get through the process are a tribute not only to the student but to the sheer plasticity of the human mind. Yet it is valuable to ask both what have we gained from the process and what have we lost.

It is hard to believe that this conversion in thinking did not occur without some fundamental change in our overall perceptual approach to other types of problem solving: specifically, the types of problem solving necessary to make effective business choices, manage and lead, and respond to change.

Ironically—and thankfully—in the process of learning how to think like lawyers, we also learned a most magnificent skill: We learned how to learn. We became autodidactic.

Remembering Richard…

In my first year of law school, as I got to know my classmates, I couldn't help but notice that most of them were pretty smart people. In college, there was a mix of people; in law school it was different—not many artistic types lugged around hornbooks or briefing cases. Most law students were logic driven thinkers.

But one student in particular stood out. He was a New Yorker named Richard, and he spoke with a very thick Brooklyn accent. He was a cross between Attorney Barry Scheck and Lieutenant Columbo. He briefed cases in the way a detective would approach a crime scene. He wanted to know everything—every fact seemed to have significance.

Richard was always asking questions in class, prodding through issues. If something didn't make sense, he would stop the class and start asking questions until it did. He didn't care about looking good—and most of the time he didn't. He just wanted to understand the reasoning behind every ruling.

At first, many of us felt sorry for Richard. His questions seemed awkward and too elementary to have much significance. He clearly wasn't getting it. In front of the entire class, he would struggle through his thinking. Unlike most of us, who made "hiding out" in class a fine art, Richard was constantly exploring the nuances of legal decisions. He would actually work through the facts of a case out loud until he understood it, and when he did, he smiled like a Jedi warrior.

Initially, some of us thought he might be losing his mind. Some doubted he would even make it through the midyear exams. Yet as the weeks and months passed, Richard's questions became more interesting and sophisticated. We could actually see his intellect transforming. His mind was being shaped to think like a lawyer's. Before long, we all wanted to know what Richard thought about a particular ruling or a point of law. Richard was a walking hornbook. In the end, he was at the very top of the class, and he became an extremely successful lawyer.

Left Brain/Right Brain

It was no coincidence that most of my classmates were heavy left-brain thinkers. The law school entrance examination ensures that left-hemisphere dominant thinkers achieve the highest scores and, therefore, have a better chance of admission to law school.

For those students who managed to get into law school with a healthy mix of right and left-hemisphere skills—hybrids, I call them—the sheer rigor of three years of law school helped them to develop skills that they perhaps would not otherwise have had. Interestingly, I have seen these types of lawyers move on to have brilliant careers, both inside and outside the field of law. In recent years, law schools have been urged to broaden their admissions policies to allow for a more mentally diverse group of students.

In the early 1990s, a lot was written about the right and left hemispheres of the brain. Researchers sought to attribute right and left-brain dominance to specific types of mental functions—even specific personality types.

It was first thought that the brain's left hemisphere exclusively managed language, linear sequencing and logic-based functions, while the right hemisphere exclusively managed intuition, visualization and creative functions.

In the past few years, however, the left-/right-hemisphere theory has been found too simplistic to be accurate. Scientists today believe that our brains have a highly distributive capacity. That is, the singular functions, such as logic and visualization—once thought to reside in either the right or the left hemisphere (but not both)—actually operate in numerous areas throughout the brain.

Through the use of modern imaging devices, we are learning that the right hemisphere, with the help of the left hemisphere, seems to perceive reality as a whole, while the left, with help from the right, seems to perceive reality through specific experiences. Combined, the two hemispheres provide us with different ways of understanding our world.

Oliver Wendell Holmes once said, "One's mind, once stretched by a new idea, never regains its original dimensions." The great Justice intuitively understood then what modern science now confirms—that the mind has an extraordinary capacity to reshape and stretch because of the very thoughts we think. Indeed, our greatest strength might come from our ability to transition from one domain to another, as difficult as this might first seem to us.

We may have been taught to think in a specific way when we were up-and-coming students in law school. We may have firmly rooted ourselves in our chosen domain without any desire—or expectation—that we would ever have to expand our minds beyond the comfortable but rigid limits of that domain. But we are fully capable of changing the way we think at any time.

The age-old expression "You can't teach an old dog new tricks" has long since yielded to scientific evidence to the contrary. We used to think that the brain slowly withered away in midlife. Science is now finding this to be untrue.

As time progresses, the brain continues to become more complex and is increasingly capable of greater degrees of plasticity. Unlike other organs that wear out with use, the brain actually grows stronger and functions at higher levels the more it is used. Our minds change and grow every time we interact with the world.

It is now scientific fact, not fiction, that changing the way we think can actually create new neural pathways resulting in new mental skills and perceptions. Our neurons are said to be in constant search of connections, ever widening the neural bandwidth of our perception.

The human mind is equipped to continually rewire itself and learn. Whenever we solve a problem creatively or force our mind to think differently, we expand the mind's physical connections. Learning new skills in new ways develops new neural connections.

In 1996 a study showed that when blind people read Braille, it activates not only the neurons that control touch, but also the part of the brain devoted to vision. Incredibly, the very neurons that are hard-wired for vision can actually rewire themselves for touch! This is good news for attorneys who fear that it may be impossible for them to learn to think like entrepreneurs.

Changing a point of view is barely a challenge to a brain that can rewire fingertips for sight.

Learning to think in new ways is not only essential for attorneys, but it is well within our grasp. Law school has sharpened our minds. It has trained us to think in certain ways. But it has also taught us to use our brains to make our way in the world.

As lawyers, we have uncommon resources at our disposal. These resources give us the capacity to make rapid progress toward achieving our goals. The way we think gives us a tremendous advantage. It is surpassed only by who we are inside.

The Self Inside the Lawyer

With his own inimitable wisdom, Justice Oliver Wendell Holmes articulated the crux of the matter when he said, "What lies behind us and what lies before us are tiny matters, compared to what lies within us…" Our thoughts, perceptions and interpretations are so thoroughly affected

by what lies within us that it behooves us to take a closer look. We need a clear awareness of the powerful influence of the self inside. Otherwise, we may miss the difference between what actually happens and what interpretation we give it. Consider the following war story:

> *It was my first trial. I was representing a woman who had slipped and fallen. Her injuries were soft tissue. She testified that she had been treated by numerous doctors but had been unable to obtain relief.*
>
> *She testified that her pain had prevented her from being able to run. She explained to the jury that running was her way of letting off steam.*

During closing, I was blackboarding the damages. When I got to pain and suffering, I chalked up about $230,000. Even before I had finished writing down this number, I noticed from the corner of my eye the first juror in the front row. She was shaking her head no. The juror, in her eighties, appeared offended that I would even suggest such a dollar amount.

I was shaken. How could I have had the audacity to ask for so much money? This was a soft tissue slip and fall, not a drowning! This eighty-year-old juror was not buying it and it was painfully obvious. I was very upset with myself.

A friend of mine, who had come down to watch the trial, saw what I had seen and quickly ran out to buy me a roll of antacids.

The jury was out for only a few hours. When they returned, that juror couldn't even look at me. I wanted to kick myself for not taking the $15,000 offer. So it came as a complete surprise to me when the foreman read the verdict: The jury had given my client the six figures we requested.

After the jury was excused, I went over to speak to the juror and asked her why she had squirmed when I wrote the dollar figure on the board. She looked at me and, in a very serious tone, told me, "Young man, I play golf every week. That game is everything to me. When she told us she couldn't run anymore…well, you couldn't give me a million dollars to give up my game. Your client deserved much more…"

The Lawyer Personality

In the mid-nineties, the Altman Weil consulting group conducted a survey of ABA members to learn whether lawyers possess specific, identifiable personality traits. While lawyers are a diverse group who come from a broad range of socioeconomic backgrounds, it soon became clear that, in regard to personality traits, they were more alike than different.

Altman Weil used the Myers-Briggs system, which has been widely used as a tool to understand and distinguish between types of personalities. It is not a clinical test. It does not qualitatively measure the status of one's mental health. Instead, it offers a way for people to recognize the ways in which they perceive their internal and external worlds.

People perceive their worlds in different ways, from different domains. Yet some go through life believing that everyone sees the world as they do. Not only is this narcissistic, but it is also scientifically inaccurate. We must, therefore, learn how to think beyond our own interpretations and learn to see the world through our clients' eyes. But let's begin by seeing what the world looks like through the eyes of lawyers.

Under the Myers-Briggs system it is believed there are at least sixteen separate personality types. Viewed this way, it could be said there are at least sixteen identifiable ways (and probably thousands more variations) of interpreting and responding to our world, at least within the context of defined personality types. Accordingly, it has been said that most lawyers fall within at least four category types: thinking, judging, introversion and sensing. In lawyers, these four types are coupled in the following ways.

Thinking/Judging
The vast majority of lawyers are considered "thinking/judging" types. Of the two, *thinking* is the more pervasive trait.

Unlike *feeling* types, who make decisions on an emotional basis, *thinking* types tend to objectify what they perceive and make decisions from a highly structured sense of logic.

Almost 80 percent of lawyers surveyed are said to be guided in their work by logical abstractions rather than emotions. Lawyers tend to think their way through problems rather than being guided by their feelings. As problem solvers, lawyers believe there is little they cannot accomplish by using intense levels of logic-based thinking. This often results in lawyers viewing people, events and things abstractly, within a logical and analytical framework.

Lawyers are also considered "judgers," according to Myers-Briggs tests. Judgers tend to thrive on procedure, established guidelines, rules and routines. The "thinking/judging" combination thrives on order, structure and intensive levels of planning.

Introversion/Sensing

Approximately 20 percent of lawyers are said to be the "introvert/sensing" type. This personality seeks out privacy, is almost always highly reserved and prefers to think through ideas alone. Yet when "introversion/sensing" is present in a personality that also has the "thinking/judging" mix, it produces a person who becomes highly energized by focusing internally.

These types of people are focused on learning from the physical world. They are intensely practical and insist on seeing tangible results from their activities. They are said to be less interested in abstractions and more interested in analyzing data.

No matter what their personality type, it is clear that lawyers are highly active thinkers. The question is whether our thinking is limited by our interpretations or whether we have the ability to reshape our thinking, learn new perspectives and thereby effectively navigate new and different domains.

When we find ourselves limited by our own perspectives, what holds us back? What prevents us from going further? Ourselves. Our domain of law, while often challenging and sometimes troubling, has grown both familiar and comfortable to us. We have worked long and hard to think like lawyers. But in the process, to some degree, we ourselves have become the barrier between where we are and where we wish to be.

Yet self-determination is only possible through the process of selfexamination. If we are to learn how to lead, manage and market, it is an absolute necessity to apply our self-determination to the challenge of developing new perspectives and learning new domains.

Moving Beyond Our Interpretations

Lawyers have an enormous capacity to learn and think. By taking the time to examine and understand *how* we think and to study different ways of thinking, we can step outside of the proverbial box.

Lawyers need to go beyond the limits set by their own interpretations. For years marketers have talked about the effect of attitude on the quality of our performance. View any challenge from the vantage point of potential gain, and chances are, the action you take will yield superior results. The opposite can be said as well. Anticipate defeat and loss and that's what you can count on.

Thankfully, the mind possesses enormous plasticity. We are *not* just the sum total of our thoughts. We are much more. We have the power to shape the very way we think and view the world. Only the human mind possesses such a skill. It is the power to choose who we wish to become by choosing how we think. This requires a conscious and determined effort—as did learning how to think like lawyers.

Select Your Point of View with Care

Lawyers need to reach a different level of thinking—not merely extend their existing knowledge base. We are not interested in knowing more of what we already know but in learning entirely new ways of thinking in entirely new areas that are powerful enough to change our actions at a fundamental level.

Science has found that our thoughts and, in particular, our beliefs can shape our experience and, therefore, our actions. Ironically, what is now being proven by science has been intuitively known by great thinkers for centuries.

Goethe wrote, "Man is made by his belief. As he believes, so he is." And over two thousand years ago the Buddha said, "The thought manifests as the word; the word manifests as the deed; the deed develops into character. So watch the thought and its ways with care…"

As suggested throughout this book, the types of mental skills that make you particularly skilled at law can work to your detriment when it comes to leading, managing and building a successful practice. Like the carpenter who sees solutions only through his hammer and nails, lawyers tend to see solutions through use of their linear-based logic.

Language and Perception

Over the last few years, a debate has raged among neuroscientists—mostly between neurolinguists and neuropsychologists. Neurolinguists argue that language frames our perceptions, while neuropsychologists argue that our perceptions shape our language. Perhaps both are right.

In any event, the intertwining of language and perception can have a remarkable effect on our professional lives. Consider how the directional component reflected in language mimics how the mind views its world. "Looking ahead" is said to be preferable to "looking back." "On the way up" is said to be superior to "on the way down." "Thinking big" is preferred to "thinking small."

Language can drive our points of view in relation to how we approach different types of challenges. We say that we look "forward" when we reference the "future" and we look "back" when we reference the "past." In the left column of Figure 5.1 (next page) are what could be considered past-based points of view, and in the right column are future-based points of view. Let's look at both extremes.

We must also consider the concept of of *selective perception*—not only, for example, whether a glass is seen as half full or half empty, but also whether we're looking at a big glass or a small glass. How we choose to perceive the glass is our decision. If we act upon our perceptions and selectively perceive things as insufficient and small, then that is what we tend to find, and the opposite is also true.

The simple truth is that thinking like a lawyer is inconsistent with building and managing a thriving enterprise, where we will be taking risks and welcoming mistakes, opening boundaries, being proactive and creative, and living in the possibility of our visions. This is a different sort of domain from that of trying cases, and to succeed, we must remove our lawyer hats and put on our entrepreneur hats. If being an excellent lawyer who is also an excellent entrepreneur is something you really desire, take comfort in knowing that you are totally capable of getting it.

FIGURE 5.1: Past and Future-Based Views

PAST-BASED VIEWS	FUTURE-BASED VIEWS
Language	**Language**
I have to...	I choose to...
It can't be done.	Let's do it this way
If only I did...	I will...
Phraseology	**Phraseology**
I see barriers...	I see opportunity...
I'm doing it all backwards!	My life is in front of me...
I won't do that again...	I'm moving ahead...
I'm going down for the count...	I'm headed for the top...
Sample Traits	**Sample Traits**
Reactive	Proactive
Sees obstacles	Sees opportunities
Resists risk	Accepts risk
Avoids change	Embraces change
Tradition driven	Choice driven
Left-Brain Driven	**Right-Brain Driven**
Memory driven	Creative driven
Logic driven	Emotion driven

Let's take this idea one step further. For argument's sake, let's suppose you're the type of person who tends to see a glass as half full (very unlikely, if you're a left-brain-dominated lawyer). Whether you see a glass as half empty or half full is important, but remember that there is another valuable insight to consider: The *size* of the glass determines the size of the risk we are willing to undertake.

If we say that we are the type of people who want to take on huge challenges, especially in our professional lives, then we will need to see *both* a large glass and one that is definitely half full.

We must understand that if we choose to take on small challenges, the risks will be small but so will the rewards. It's the proverbial dilemma of wanting big things but thinking too small to get them. This type of thinking is fundamentally inconsistent.

If you're out to reinvent your law firm, you will need to look through a new set of lenses—you will need to see the glass as both large and half full. So, *choose a challenge worthy of your ambitions.*

In *The Master Game*, Robert S. de Ropp wrote: "Life games reflect life aims." A great example of this is Michael Jordan. When Jordan tried playing professional baseball, many thought it was an act of arrogance. Some ridiculed him for daring: "Who does he think he is? Just because he was great in basketball, what gives him the right to think he'll be great in baseball?"

He wasn't, but that's not what is important here. The point is that great athletes like Jordan freely choose to take risks even while they are at the top of their game. In contrast, most of us choose the safety and comfort of success rather than exposing ourselves to the possibility of defeat. We get so stuck in our own success that we stop taking aim at our goals and consequently we find ourselves out of the game.

Therefore, if you choose to take on small challenges, expect *small* rewards and *small* disappointments. There is nothing wrong with choosing small challenges. People live their lives like this every day. However, it's both naïve and silly to expect large rewards when the challenges we undertake are small.

Likewise, if we take on *large* challenges, we can expect large rewards and yes, sometimes, *large* disappointments. They are opposite sides of the same coin. However, what is critical to recognize is that whether we choose to play small or play big is entirely up to us. It's our choice.

In order to make your professional life as fulfilling as possible, you must build a firm that will soar. Know that in doing this, you've chosen to play a big game that will take great strength and courage.

You will need to jump high and take careful aim—follow through on your shot and don't take your eyes off the basket until you hear the swish of the ball through the net.

And remember, the way you *think* about your game is how you will end up playing it.

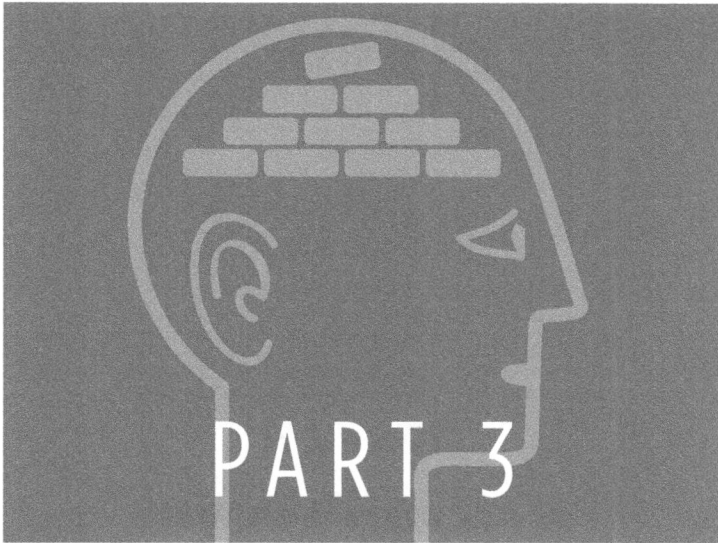

PART 3

Reinventing Your Firm

*"Greatness
is not where we stand
but in what direction
we are moving."*

OLIVER WENDELL HOLMES

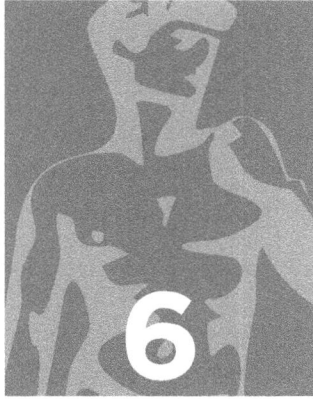

The Art of Firm Sculpting

An ancient story tells of a student who sought to learn from his master the secret of becoming a great sculptor.

"Master," the student said, " I want to make a great and beautiful statue, but I do not know the methods of your great work."

The master replied, "What exactly do you seek to make?"

The student paused, and then said, "I seek to sculpt a most beautiful elephant."

The master then pointed a few feet away to a large block of stone and a mallet and chisel. "That is your marble and those are your tools. All you have to do now is carve away everything that does not look like a beautiful elephant."

When I first read this story, I thought about how frustrating this experience might have felt for this poor student. How would any of us know what was not a beautiful elephant? How would we know, at first, what to keep and what to carve away?

Only after many careful strokes of the chisel against the stone can sculptors begin to see their visions take form. Likewise, it requires great effort and determination to match our visions to reality, so we must begin by knowing both: not only what we wish to create, but also what exists now—what separates the vision from the reality.

Know Thy Firm

One way to begin sculpting a new firm is to picture your *ideal* firm in your mind's eye. The goal, of course, is to carve that vision into existence—to chisel down to that beautiful elephant which, for the moment, is hidden from your view. Firm sculpting is all about finding and articulating what is hidden.

Creating a whole new culture cannot be done halfheartedly. You wouldn't expect to reveal a beautiful elephant by making a few random chips into the stone from time to time, hoping for the best. Likewise, you can't dabble or tinker your way to effecting firm-wide change. While the chiseling begins on the exterior, what emerges from deep within the firm's core are the inspired values of the firm's leadership. Firm sculpting is the process of removing everything that is not your ideal vision of the firm.

One partner I spoke with had approached the issue of change by having the firm's stationery redesigned, hiring a few new lawyers and buying new furniture for the staff. He even changed the color of the walls and installed a speaker system that played music in the hallways.

Needless to say, while some at the firm enjoyed the new vibe, the changes were superficial at best. This partner made the common mistake of trying to effect change from the outside in rather than from the inside out.

A "tinkering" approach will not create lasting change; a profoundly different approach is needed.

Surprisingly, most partners I spoke with agreed with this notion completely. A partner of a midsize San Francisco firm shared this observation:

> *We all read the latest and greatest practice management books. They all talk about meaningful change. We're not*

naïve. We all want the same thing. But after it's all said and done, we're still doing the same things in the same ways as before...

Developing New Questions

The point here is to not focus on what you already know, but on what you *don't* know. This is accomplished not by finding a new set of answers to the same types of questions, but by finding different questions that will lead to new insights and new ways of thinking. Conventional questions generate conventional answers, which will lead to the same place you are now.

In order to create fundamental change, you must move from the familiar to the unfamiliar. New thinking requires a new mind-set and a new context. New perspectives require new levels of questioning that will encourage you to shake loose from old barriers and self-imposed limits.

Said another way, we need to alter our inquiry by changing our mental reference point, and this requires thinking about *how* we think. Again the neurosciences offer us new and valuable insights.

Our capacity for knowledge and variation is astonishing. Neuroscientists believe that our minds have reached less than a third of their evolutionary capacity and that they are developing at a faster rate today than at any time in our history (see *A User's Guide to the Brain* by John Ratey, M.D.). There has never been a better time for us to embrace new ways of thinking and relating to others—our brains are primed for it.

Legal reasoning works best in closed systems, where there are accepted rules and outcomes. But in our quest to build a firm that is profoundly different, we cannot be constrained by such rules. Responding successfully to change demands that we cultivate more than logic if we want to thrive. We must encourage and foster intuition and creativity to discover new ways of approaching problems and new rules that will make it possible to adapt to the unexpected forces of change.

It's true that rational thought works best within the boundaries of rational systems like law, where we rely on a stable foundation of rules and processes.

Clearly, in this environment, it works to have rational, logical structures by which to model our thinking.

But our brains have the capacity for so much more. No matter how accustomed we become to thinking within the closed system of a particular domain, we are constantly engaged in dynamic mental processes that maintain the remarkable agility of our minds.

If you doubt the capacity of even the most stolid, unimaginative member of your firm to think in new ways, consider this:

In everyday speech, the number of different types of sentences an ordinary person is able to produce is astounding. Let's assume a person is able to formulate a sentence made up of just twenty words, such as the first sentence of this paragraph. The number of different types of sentences a person could be expected to formulate with these cognitive abilities can be expressed mathematically as 1020—or a hundred-million trillion different sentence variations.

The limits of our memory are unknown. But we do know that the mind of an average college graduate can process and store up to ten thousand distinct pictures without any attempt to memorize them—and then, within a few days, recognize those pictures with more than 90 percent accuracy.

Compared to the commonplace feats of versatility your mind exhibits every day, the challenge of developing new questions about your firm seems much more manageable. And it is well within the capacity of your firm if it is willing to consider the possibilities. Consider what it might mean if you were able to reinvent your firm from values that inspired you as well as your firm's leadership.

The Illusion of the Status Quo

Getting others to recognize their capacity for change is not always easy. Alan Perskin, a managing partner in a firm with more than seventy lawyers, described his frustration with his partners: "Without real change, this firm is slowly heading for extinction. Most of our partners are in denial. They ignore all the warning signs and give only lip service when the other partners come up with new ideas. They don't like change. They are married to the old ways of doing things, even if it means the rest of the profession is passing us by."

It is easier to resist change than to engage it. Unfortunately, most people develop themselves around goals that lead to stagnation rather than growth. People tend to first view change as threatening rather than empowering. This is especially true in larger firms, where people tend to think job security is contingent on maintaining the status quo.

Both inside and outside the firm, people avoid rocking the boat. Maintaining the status quo, however, is simply a way to avoid change and justify stagnation. The reality is that *change* is the only constant. Nothing stands still—not even law firms. You either move forward toward your goals or give in to inertia and drift backward. The backward movement may occur slowly. You may not be able to see it, but it is taking place.

Resisting change is normal for most people and, therefore, for most organizations. It is a form of complacency—it comes upon us like slow death, and all too often we can't see its results until it's too late. Then all we can do is try to pick up the pieces.

If you embark on a mission to change your firm, you must understand the serious nature of change. You need to know the playing field—not just at the organizational level, but at a visceral and emotional level.

Change, like time, cannot be suppressed or made to stand still. Often our resistance to change is motivated by nothing more than our fear of not knowing what the outcome will be. Yet change is as natural as growing older. It happens whether we like it or not and whether we know it or not.

Whether or not an opportunity for change exists and, if such an opportunity exists, whether it appears as a daunting barrier or an appealing challenge, depends more upon the mind-set of the person confronting it than on objective material conditions. What is needed, therefore, is a keen sense of clarity in your approach to change.

Why We Need Clarity

The visions you create today will become your firm's traditions tomorrow. Creating new traditions in the face of resistance and stagnation takes a very clear sense of purpose.

You need not only to see *where* you are going, but also to know *why* you're going there. And when you get there, you will need to know *what* will happen next. Thus, clarity of purpose within your firm must be aggressively managed—and it must reach every member of the firm.

Law firms, like any other enterprise confronted with the need to change, are faced with the challenge of re-creating themselves or risking being stuck in the dormancy of stagnation—trapped in the legacy of someone else's firm, someone else's traditions, someone else's dreams. Intelligent and wellintentioned people—even those with great financial wealth—can find themselves living their professional lives in quiet desperation.

If this thought is not repulsive to you, then consider whether you have become so resigned to the way your professional life is now that broader issues no longer seem relevant, important or even possible. The fact is, you are well into completing this book, which says more about you than you might realize. It demonstrates your openness and makes a bold statement that you are not willing to settle for more of the same in a profession that is screaming out for a new, more vital form of leadership.

Steps to Achieving Change

You may be saying to yourself, "I can't do this alone. In fact, I'm not even sure I'm in a sufficiently powerful position within the firm to initiate this kind of change." You may be right. Changing the firm's culture requires the enrollment of as many of the firm's influential members as possible. Without a strong consensus among the firm's top leadership that fundamental change is necessary in order for the firm to grow and prosper, the chances of effecting such change will be extremely slim.

A professional facilitator can serve as an objective outside observer whose very presence is a validation of the idea that it's time for change. Most members of your firm's leadership are probably too close to the firm's problems to see them from new perspectives. A skilled facilitator will have a strong background in the field of law and experience in marketing and management—and will, ideally, be able to command the respect of the firm's leaders and convince them that change is necessary for survival.

The facilitator is not embroiled in the firm's politics and, consequently, does not get mired down in internal power plays; nor does he or she allow personality differences among the leaders to affect the process of change. The facilitator's job is to make sure that the right systems are in place, that the process is paced properly and that it runs smoothly. The facilitator helps to identify the firm's blind spots while never pronouncing judgment or assigning blame. A skilled, experienced facilitator has only one agenda: to serve and support the leadership in bringing about the changes they seek.

The Five Stages Toward Reinvention

Each of these stages will be discussed in more depth, but for now, they are summarized so that the contextual framework of the change process can be better understood.

1. *A Search for Leadership*
2. *Forming Your Inner Team*
3. *Finding Your Firm's Vision*
4. *Drafting Your Firm's Master Charter*
   (and Creating Derivative Charters)
5. *Bringing the Rest on Board*
   (and Creating Strategic Action Plans)

The first two stages are usually, but not always, under way before the facilitator is invited into the process. Sometimes, though, the facilitator is asked to consult early on to offer insight into the initial stages of forming the inner circle of people who will lead the primary charge. Usually these partners already know who they are and are prepared to move forward with the process.

1. Search for Leadership

True leaders have the capacity to articulate a vision and inspire others to pursue it with them. True leaders come from a place of honesty—with willingness to see what actually *is* and discover what *could be* through community effort. They bring with them a confidence that gives others the courage to strive for even the loftiest goals.

Your firm's potential for change lies in the hands of such a true leader. Without a strong individual with the skill to push for change by enlisting rather than alienating others, your firm may make important improvements, but it is unlikely to reach its full potential.

The all-important first step in initiating change is to find such a leader within your ranks. Once *you* are committed to seeing things change, look around and ask yourself who will lead. (The answer may be as close as your own reflection in a mirror.)

Once the leader is chosen, whether he's the partner with the most power and seniority in the firm or a more junior partner who is eager and willing to support the process, his or her first step is to identify and enlist the other key players in your firm.

2. Forming Your Inner Team (the Key Partners)

The next step is to identify the principal members of the team—the inner circle. Most of the time, the inner circle will be composed of key partners and, in some firms, top-level administrators. Without them on board, the probability of creating profound change at the root level is seriously diminished. Bring them on board as soon as possible.

But before the firm does this, it must address a very serious issue. It must know whether the core power base—the inner circle—includes what is referred to as a "Toxic Partner." Like a drop of poison in a carafe, a single "Toxic" can be fatal to even the most brilliant and ambitious of plans. (More on dealing with Toxics can be found in Chapter 8.)

3. Finding Your Firm's Vision

Once the leader and the inner circle have been identified and any Toxics have been dealt with, the next step is for your leader to set up a series of meetings to determine what the firm's values and challenges are and then begin to articulate a vision for the firm's future. Ideally, a facilitator will be brought in at this point to help keep things on track.

Uncovering your firm's values is no easier than confronting its challenges. Your firm's values must inspire the partners if there is any hope of inspiring the firm itself and its clients. When the members of the inner circle envision the firm, they should identify which values move and inspire them. These inspired values must appeal to them at a visceral level, not just sound good. Left to their own devices, many partners (and professional marketers) come up with meaningless phrases like "We live to serve." Your firm's inspired values must be held to a higher standard than this.

The values must be concrete and measurable; the first measure is whether they elicit a positive emotional reaction that motivates action. You'll know when the values defined by the inner circle are powerful enough—endorphins will kick in, enthusiasm will rise and it will inspire people to take action.

4. Drafting Your Firm's Master Charter (and Creating Derivative Charters)

The inspiration and commitment achieved during the first seminal meetings will soon be evidenced in the creation of your firm's *master charter*. As will be discussed in much more detail in later chapters, it is the inspired values and principles found in the master charter that will guide what we call *derivative charters*—charters that belong to your key departments, practice groups and committees.

The master charter must be anchored in the leadership's inspired values. It is the first evidence of what has been a dynamic, proactive process. The master charter must be real, not contrived. It must be rooted in the leadership's intentions for the firm and the principles on which the firm will be governed from now on.

The master charter will become the focal point of the firm's identity. It is the document that articulates the inspired values and priorities of the firm. It will not be drafted in a day—creating it takes introspection, analysis, debate and thoughtful examination. But when it is finished, it is the equivalent of a *constitution* for your firm. If it is done with excellence, it will both guide and inspire every member of your firm to actions that are congruent with the firm's identity.

Once a powerful firm culture is in place, the master charter's norms and values will keep the firm on the path to following its inspired values and will discourage individual or group conduct that is inconsistent with those values.

Once the master charter is completed, many law firms falter. The leadership becomes excited about the new charter and circulates it among the other members of the firm. A few memos go out touting the power of vision and describing the bright future that lies ahead. A few of the more ambitious partners try to rally the troops around the cause, but soon the inspiration begins to pale and the charter fades into the background, with no more appeal than the firm's letterhead and logo.

Resculpting is for naught unless the people below the leadership level believe that the vision is relevant to their lives. I can't emphasize this enough: *The relevance cannot be illusory; it must be as real to them as their weekly paycheck.* So your next step *must be* to give them both the responsibility *and* the authority to put changes into action.

In order to do this, I recommend that the firm's charter be a jumping-off point from which each major department creates its own charter and plan of action (more on these strategic action plans in number 5 below) within the vision that the leadership has delineated. These derivative charters and the strategic action plans will give the members of the firm a personal stake in their future.

The facilitator, with the support of top leadership, must ensure that each of the firm's major departments, practice groups and committees is given time and support in crafting these all-important documents. Otherwise the subordinates will perpetually feel that this is the leadership's vision, not theirs. Giving them the opportunity to participate is the only way to make the vision relevant, and it will also make them accountable for the results.

The challenge lies in getting the inspiration and enthusiasm evoked by the creation of the new vision to truly motivate *everyone*—all the way down to the people on the lowest rungs of the firm's ladder. The solution is to *empower* everyone. Skipping this step will undermine all of the firm's efforts.

In the end, every member of the firm should be enrolled in the change process. Every member of the firm who comes into contact with clients, vendors, other firms' attorneys, or anyone else should reflect the firm's inspired values and identity. Every form of marketing, advertising and promotion should be inseparably integrated with the people who make up the firm.

5. Bringing the Rest on Board (and Creating Strategic Action Plans)

This last step in reinventing the firm happens once the master charter and derivative chapters are written. To allow everyone in the firm to take part— to take ownership—in the changes the firm is making, the leaders of each of the firm's major departments, committees and practice groups, in conjunction with each of their respective team members, will construct detailed action plans that identify specific goals, specify time lines and names of people accountable for bringing the goals to fruition. These strategic action plans should be developed for each of the major departments in the firm.

Strategic action plans are developed only *after* the firm's charter and the derivative charters have been carved out by the leadership. These charters are the basis for the strategic action plans, which are tangible instructions for making decisions and taking action.

Strategic action plans can be thought of as logical extensions of the firm's values and beliefs. They are, by nature, imbued with the firm's culture. They can take on enormous momentum, capable of pushing the firm forward to new heights and performance levels.

Strategic action plans bridge the gap between the firm's words and its deeds. They provide specific task-driven objectives against which the firm's leadership, including the managers, can test assumptions and gauge the firm's departmental performance.

The single most important characteristic of strategic action plans is that they are task-specific—they describe purposes, time lines and responsibilities for the tasks the firm performs. These plans, as well as the specific goals they are intended to achieve, must in the end be measured against both the derivative and master charters.

• • •

Although it is never easy to challenge the status quo or achieve fundamental change within an organization, the personal and professional rewards are boundless. Moving away from a firm's preconceived notions frees it from existing limitations. The vision that emerges from the process of sculpting your firm allows your firm to create a new identity that will greatly increase client satisfaction and propel the firm's success.

7

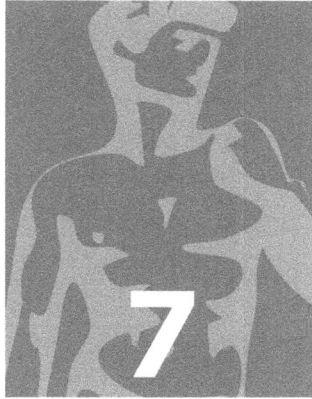

A Search for Leadership

There is a wonderful children's book entitled *Are You My Mother?* It's about a chick that hatches and falls from its nest, never having seen its mother. The chick does not know what it looks like or even that it is a chick.

It has no way of knowing anything about itself.

Without its mother, the chick has no identity. Without an identity, the chick is lost. The chick asks a dog whether it is his mother; a tree, whether it is his mother. The chick even asks a tractor if *it* is his mother.

Often a search for identity includes a profound search for a leader— that special person whom you can count on to protect you and show you the way to better times.

The Partner Pole

In ancient times the totem pole was a symbolic expression of past generations. It offered information about a tribe's identity—a type of linear understanding of generations that came before them and the leaders who showed them the way. It enforced group solidarity and provided a necessary relational context to their lives.

The totem pole was worshiped and ritualized. The history of a whole tribe could be understood by this one linear expression.

Symbolic communication, as a group organizing method, is also found in law firms. Law firms proudly list their partners' names on letterhead and post them on doorways. Often some of the names are symbols of the past— a lasting recognition of those who came before as well as those who are currently carrying the torch of the firm's traditions into the future.

This symbolic communication portrays the history of a firm's leadership and is an indicator of predicted performance.

But what happens when the firm's past is forced to yield to the firm's future? When it becomes necessary for the firm to reinvent itself and set out new organizing principles that match its vision—when the old belief system is no longer in sync with the needs and demands of changing markets and clients?

Most firms are facing this challenge right now, and some are not even aware of it. The partners I spoke with clearly recognized the need to reinvent themselves or risk sacrificing growth and prosperity.

You the Leader?

Who among you will lead the charge? This is a very personal decision that should not be taken lightly. It will depend not only on your own willingness to take on the challenge, but also on the willingness of the key partners who make up most of the power base at your firm.

If you are up for the challenge, accept this knowledge and get on with leading. If not, find the person in your firm who is ready and able to lead and offer that person all the support you can. You'll soon realize that the quality and commitment of your support for this person will be recognized as an important form of leadership in its own right.

Genetics of Leadership

It's been said that some people are born leaders. That may be true, but for most of us, leadership is an acquired skill that comes from our mind-set and our desire to effect positive change. Similarly, people are not born extraordinary. Instead, they choose to accomplish extraordinary things.

As recently as 2003, scientists discovered that our natural traits are not "set in stone." (See Matt Ridley's *Genome* and *Nature via Nurture*.) Rather, our genetic code—especially the code responsible for our brain function—is neither unchanging nor unchangeable. As we respond to the challenges and stimuli in the world, so do our genes. Depending upon our needs and the degree of our determination, different formulations of our genetic code are activated. This results in the emergence of a new pattern of genetic instructions. Contrary to what scientists formerly believed, our genes remain active, malleable and fluid throughout our lives.

Until these discoveries were made, the received wisdom was that the traits that enable us to think like lawyers or strive for excellence or find the courage and charisma to lead were handed out to us—or not—at birth. It was taken as fact that our neural makeup was primarily dictated by the genetic code we inherited from our parents. If we were fortunate enough to have inherited "smart" genes, it was anticipated that we were destined for greatness; if the opposite happened, we were destined to be the village idiot.

In reality, the reason so few of us break out of the mold is not due to genetics at all. It's because of the fact that, strange as it may sound, most of us surrender to our strengths rather than engage our weaknesses. If we tend to be naturally gifted in mathematics, we gravitate toward mathematics. If we show an early talent in the arts, we gravitate in that direction. It's simply easier to rely on our existing strengths than it is to develop new strengths from scratch. Psychologist and theorist Carl Jung described this irony in his book *Psychological Types*:

> *[E]xperience shows that it is hardly possible... for anyone to bring all his psychological functions to simultaneous development. The very conditions of society enforce a man to apply himself first and foremost to the differentiation of that function with which he is either most gifted by nature, or which provides his most effective means for social success.*

Very frequently, indeed as a general rule, a man identifies himself more or less completely with the most favored, hence the most developed function.

Since Jung's time, however, neuroscientists have discovered that the human tendency to follow the path of least resistance is not merely ironic but counterproductive. We now know that the brain grows stronger, developing at a much higher level, when we force ourselves to think in new and different ways.

Until now, you may not have thought of yourself as a leader. But that is no reason to believe you can't become one if your motivation is strong enough. The first question to ask yourself is this: *What does it mean to be a leader?*

A Leader

The stereotypical image of a leader is that of a commanding figure, able to speak to large groups of people. We think of leaders as people who speak their minds and are charismatic performers, able to manipulate people's emotions in order to get things done the right way—usually their way.

This popular stereotype is not only unrealistic, it describes characteristics that are undesirable in a leader and, if we dare to admit it, characteristics that make a leader quite dysfunctional. Real leaders are listeners; they don't bark out orders from behind their desks. Such leaders find ways to develop strengths in the people they work with. They work through people, by understanding and evoking their intelligence, creativity and participation.

The ideal leader works for the firm, not the other way around. In fact, leadership is more a property of the firm than of the leader. In mid to large size firms, it is unrealistic to rely on one person to provide all of the leadership.

The most successful managing partners I have seen rarely dominate the group; rather they support the group by keeping it focused and on task. Leaders rely on others to help them stay organized. Watch a leader and a trusted secretary interact—can you tell who is managing whom?

Exceptional leaders work hard to remove barriers in communication among their key people. They see their role as smoothing out processes. They are facilitators, not dominators. They think about ways of making others more effective and productive, making it easier for them to do their jobs. And when their effort results in success, these leaders rarely take the credit, instead giving it to the group, where it belongs.

The single most important quality people look for in a leader is honesty. For most people, this is what determines whether a leader is worthy of their confidence and loyalty. With honesty often comes wisdom.

For firms in the midst of great change, leadership requires a unique set of skills. Leaders must be able to work through teams of people, delegating work and rewarding performance while encouraging persistence. Such leaders encourage excellent performance at every level. Effective leaders are relentless in their determination to keep reaching for higher levels of performance. Interestingly, leaders like these seem to work best when the chips are down and change is upon them.

The Best Leaders Are Perspective-Driven

The most dynamic types of leader are perspective-driven. These intensely inquisitive people need to know what actually causes firms to grow and prosper and, just as importantly, what *causes* them to falter. They want to know what clients think about the firm—what clients actually experience when they visit and do business with the firm.

Perspective-driven leaders seek to discover new ways of serving, new ways of making clients feel valued, and new ways of earning trust. They seek what many managing partners would rather sweep under the rug. That's because perspective-driven leaders know that the creative process depends more on differing views than conforming ones.

A common trait of perspective-driven leaders is that they are painfully honest and realistic when it comes to evaluating performance—including their own. These leaders do not claim to have a monopoly on knowledge.

They understand that their point of view is simply that—their point of view.

They know that to completely understand a major challenge, they must turn to people who think in a variety of ways; thinking in teams is usually more productive than thinking individually.

Perspective-driven leaders do not let dissent or disagreement distract them from their goal of problem solving. In fact, such leaders are *attracted* to disagreement, especially from intelligent and competent people.

Listen to how one managing partner dealt with disagreement:

> *Most of our partners were having a major problem with our top administrator, who was insisting that we convert to an entirely new computer system. The partners couldn't see how the cost and expense of putting in a new system could*
>
> *possibly be worth the projected productivity gains. We just weren't seeing what he was seeing—and none of us were willing to make the effort to see the problem through his eyes. No one doubted he was a talented and intelligent administrator. But no one here could possibly imagine that an administrator might be seeing something that we couldn't.*
>
> *I later realized that it was our arrogance that was getting in the way. When we finally put the system in, a year later, we were kicking ourselves for not having done it earlier...*

True leaders value the *differences* among people—and more importantly, they respect those differences. The more a leader discovers what was previously unknown, the more opportunities can be identified. Leaders must be committed more to understanding the problem from another's perspective than worrying about protecting their own understanding.

Playing at Top Performance Levels

Great leaders, like great athletes, are relentless and uncompromising when it comes to reaching top performance levels. It is this tenacious desire to be the best at one's game that drives them.

Perspective-driven leaders recognize the limits of one's own perceptions and appreciate the need to interact with different types of people. They realize that people do not always see the world as it is, but tend to see it from the perspective of who they are and how they view and interact with others. This is why such leaders encourage diversity. This is why you might hear an effective leader say, "Jay, you seem to see this issue differently than I do. Tell me how you're seeing it. I want to see what you see."

Most people in management roles would rather learn from what's working at their firm than from what's not working. Typical managers seek out agreement among their coworkers rather than finding opposing views. Perspective-driven leaders seek just the opposite—they are more interested in what's missing from the firm that, if instituted, would make a qualitative difference and elevate performance.

A business litigation firm in rural New York was experiencing a serious decline in new business. When the partners got together to discuss the issue, they thought it would be useful to see what other firms were doing that they were not. Giving associates bonuses had always been discretionary, based on their overall performance. But the partners realized, when they compared their compensation packages with those of other firms, that theirs lacked a specific and immediate reward structure for associates.

One partner said, "We found that associates were especially motivated when they knew exactly what they would earn from new income they brought in and when they could expect to receive their share. We were amazed at how quickly they responded."

This firm was acting proactively. They sought not only what was working, but also what was not working in their new business efforts. When they discovered that there was a decline in associate-generated revenue, they looked at what was absent—from the associates' perspectives. Discovering what was absent allowed them to take immediate action to remedy the situation to everyone's satisfaction.

Knowing Your Game

Perspective-driven leaders consider the challenge of finding what's *not* working at their firms to be particularly interesting. That's not to say they don't acknowledge their firms' strengths, but they are much more intrigued by their weaknesses. Why? Because they understand that removing weakness builds strength and increases performance. It is like finding the beautiful elephant in the block of stone. When you eliminate what's not working (what's not the beautiful elephant), you often get closer to what is working.

For perspective-driven leaders, finding what's missing in their organization is like working a puzzle. The more pieces they find, the more complete the picture becomes and the easier it is to find the next missing piece.

It's no different from the mind-set of a great athlete—and athletes don't get any greater than Michael Jordan. Even at the height of his career, Jordan was notorious for studying his game tapes the day after he played. To him, reaching higher levels of performance meant learning as much as possible about how he played.

It wasn't vanity that drove him to study his game. It was his desire to see what he could *not* see from his perspective on the floor during a game. By changing his perspective, he could see things that he might have missed before. He might notice, for example, that in fast breaks in the last quarter of a game, he tended to pass the ball more to the left than to the right. Was this a mistake on his part? That's not the point. What great athletes like Jordan look for is more knowledge about how they play their game. It's finding that next piece of the puzzle that lets them get closer to seeing the complete picture.

Powerful Leaders Are Great Listeners

Perspective-driven leaders have many traits in common. One is being masterful at communication. This does not mean just being an effective speaker—it also means being an effective listener. The way one listens is said to be more important than what one says.

Providing consistently high levels of service requires constant listening to feedback from clients, and the people listening must be the most senior members of a firm's leadership. Unfortunately, for the more senior partners, it's too easy to avoid such listening—they become insulated from the front lines.

The inertia of this avoidance is enforced by those who wish to "protect" top leadership from unpleasant experiences such as speaking directly with dissatisfied clients. This happens in even the most well-intentioned firms. To counter it, firms must be proactive.

The best firms, for example, are obsessive about conducting in-depth debriefing sessions after a matter is concluded. These meetings are essential to ensure the firm's ability to track its progress in serving clients, and clients also appreciate and admire the firm's frank and honest willingness to improve its relationship with them.

Most leaders pretend to listen. Perspective-driven leaders, on the other hand, are fully engaged in the listening process. They are tenaciously committed to understanding the perspectives of others. To them, listening is not just waiting for someone else to finish talking or a competition between views. Nor is the goal of listening necessarily to reach agreement.

Rather, astute listening is the process of working through issues and separating the emotional from the logical while discovering more about the assumptions used to draw conclusions. Good listeners care less about being "right" than they do about building strong coalitions among their people.

Often people listen in order to validate their own replies. Few actually listen to understand another person's perspective, and even fewer try to understand the *person* behind the perspective. Listening has become a unilateral waiting game. We nod our heads to look attentive and interested, but inside we're working up a clever reply. ("Finish up, so I can tell you what I think about it!")

Sadly, most of us don't bother to really understand the people we listen to. This is not just a trait of lawyers, but lawyers in particular should not settle for how "most people" communicate. Providing legal service demands that we strive to reach a much higher standard than "most people" in interpersonal communication. It is not by chance that we are called *counselors*-at-law.

People need to be understood. This need is second only to their need to survive. They need to participate in communication that affirms and validates them as people. Listening is perhaps the single most important aspect in client communication. No matter how much time it takes, it is worth every moment. Furthermore, it is said that it is only after we listen and listen well that we earn the right to be listened to.

It is through listening that you will begin to discover what your clients truly value. Only when you know what each client—individually—values can you hope to provide them with the type of excellent service that builds loyalty and praise.

Listen to the Clients You Already Have

It is not the hundreds of *potential* clients that might one day become revenue opportunities that count. It's your *existing* clients that are your greatest assets. Investing in them by listening to them will generate your greatest return.

The traditional 80/20 rule applies to most large firms: That is, 80 percent of a firm's revenue comes from just 20 percent of its clients. So marketing well must begin with your existing clients. Listening to these clients, reassuring them and making sure that they are well-served at every level must be your first priorities.

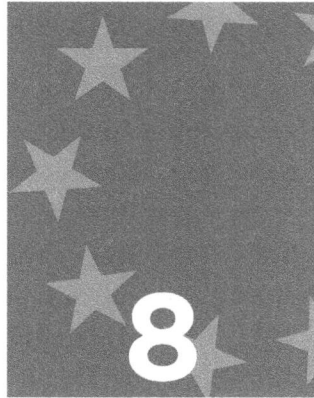

Forming Your Inner Team

Your inner team will include your firm's major partners and top administrators. Ideally, *you* are the managing partner, but this is not essential if you have the managing partner's honest support and commitment to change. In some cases, the managing partner will be your strongest ally and will do whatever it takes to help you to be successful. Remember, your success will be on the managing partner's clock—under his authority. This person— more often than not—has more to gain and less to lose than you might realize.

The inner team should be made up of people in whom you have confidence and with whom you have developed a solid relationship. They will be your support, both professionally and personally. They will be your sounding board in sharing ideas and discussing challenges.

Re-creating the firm will lead to discussing fundamental values. You must build consensus. Each member of the team must feel comfortable being open and frank with each other. To this end, the group must agree on total and absolute confidentiality. It must be agreed upon and honored that nothing may leave the room until everyone says so. I don't say this lightly—I have seen the best-laid plans fail due to loose lips.

Talking about one's aspirations and desires for change usually causes people to feel energized—even excited. Once the group starts meeting, you will be in for a few surprises. You may see emotions in your partners that you have not seen in a very long time—perhaps never.

Once team members have discussed their aspirations and desires for the firm, the second step is to uncover what your "ideal firm" might look like. Developing a description of the "ideal firm" will require each member of the team to ask what really matters, at both a personal and a professional level. How deep the team is willing to go at this point will be an important measure of how successful and pervasive your firm's transformation will be.

Some members of your team will come to the table saying they want change, but then they will spend most of their time resisting it. This is a problem. Many times this happens because the process of self-examination can be threatening. People can feel uncomfortable with the idea of giving up an image of themselves that they have spent years developing and protecting.

Describing your ideal firm will require going beyond the familiar forms of problem solving and entering the realm of reinvention and transformation.

Going Beyond Conventional Approaches

Albert Einstein wrote, "The significant problems we face cannot be solved at the same level of thinking we were at when we created them."

Conventional problem solving produces conventional results. If your aim is to profoundly change your firm's culture, you will need to toss out the old methods and try new ones. Creating a different type of firm will require a different type of thinking—one that is anchored in your imagination as opposed to your memory. Unrestricted by your past, you will be free to set goals rather than being restrained by the usual ceilings, which are often based on self-imposed limitations.

In order to stretch his own limits, Einstein practiced playing the violin—a skill that did not come naturally to him. Scientists have since discovered that engaging in unfamiliar and demanding types of thinking physically improves our neural circuitry. Whenever we cultivate previously underused neurons, our brains become more integrated and more functionally complete.

Einstein didn't have the MRIs to back it up, but he did know that when he forced himself to play the violin, he was using a different part of his brain. He found that this stimulated his ability to think creatively within his own domain of mathematics and physics. Frequently, in the middle of playing his violin, he would be inspired by a new insight and reach for his notes to solve a problem or pose a new question.

You need not be an Einstein to remodel your neural makeup. The ability to do so is an integral part of what makes us human. We can actually *think about* our thinking. This ability is what makes our mental capacity uniquely human. But we must also be willing to accept the challenge of stepping out of the linear confines of our thinking.

For some firms, the only way to respond to the challenge of reinventing the firm is to find a *new* leader—one who can think "outside the box" and inspire as many as possible within the firm to do the same.

The Size Factor

Managing partners today, unlike in the past, are called upon to demonstrate credibility on a variety of fronts, not the least of which are marketing and business leadership. The person who next takes the helm of your firm will provide important insights into both the firm's operations and its current culture. The types of skills this person must have will depend somewhat on the size of your firm.

Understandably, the nature and scope of a managing partner's role often depends on the firm's size. The larger the firm, the more problematic it is to shape the firm's direction and effect firm-wide change. But don't be fooled. Small practices are often up against the same problems.

Small Firms

For small firms, it is the partners themselves who make most decisions. The need for consensus building and bringing issues to a formal vote is less critical. Decisions tend to be made with more spontaneity and with less formality than in larger firms.

In most cases, it is easier for smaller firms to manage change and act on new opportunities than it is for larger firms. The downside is that unless the firm has some diversity in its practice areas, a change in one area can result in a strain on the firm's capital—enough so that it keeps the partners awake at night.

Midsize Firms

For midsize firms, there is usually a strong need to build consensus among partners before a major firm decision can be made. The partners will spend considerable time fact-finding and gathering information before bringing an important matter to a vote. The benefit of this is that major decisions are thoroughly examined and discussed before the firm takes action. The drawback is that the process can be frustratingly slow and drawn out, and as a result, time-critical opportunities are sometimes missed. A strong managing partner can often move the process along more quickly through leadership and strong consensus building.

Large Firms

Large firms face extraordinary challenges when reshaping themselves. Most managing partners functioning in their traditional capacities quickly realize that they cannot do it all. Consequently, management authority is handed over to numerous committees. The overall concept of the desired changes frequently becomes fragmented, and ideas that require broad-based approaches can easily be stifled by myopic thinking. Stagnation and resistance to change are rampant in these firms and are silent killers, sucking out the last ounce of the firms' vitality.

Committees are often appointed when the firm's top leadership is not willing to tackle tough decision making itself. Not only can this lead to fragmented decisions, but the decisions can also be postponed or even lost in the process. The real danger of committees is that it's possible for the role of management to be absorbed into the abyss of committee. All too often, committee members do not see themselves or function as part of a team but rather as objective observers, setting goals and passing judgment on the performance of others. They often view their roles as separate and distinct from the fray, and therefore they are rarely able to effect meaningful change. Despite all of this, most large firms believe that committees are necessary evils.

Who Will Lead the Leaders in Reshaping the Firm?

Historically, choosing the next managing partner has been a knee-jerk response. Most firms fill the void by putting in the next best rainmaker, if there ever was one. Others look for a firm workhorse or a partner with particularly strong administrative and/or financial skills. Some are a combination of these traits; others gravitate toward finding a copycat of the previous managing partner. Finding a new leader with the right combination of clout and charisma to reshape the firm is a tremendous challenge.

The Copycat

The copycat works on filling the big guy's shoes. A few personality changes here—a tuck, a fold—and the copycat thinks that in time he will be recreated in the Great One's image.

Replacing a managing partner with a copycat is destined to fail. Cloning personalities is impossible, even in laboratory rats. The reality is, only the predecessor can be predecessor—and that person has left the building. Pretending that his persona lives on through his successor is unhealthy, and and it will polarize a firm.

The Super Administrator

Perhaps the most distracting of management personalities is the super administrator. For this partner, great management means great administration. Likewise, leadership is measured by the proper allocation of yellow-pad spending or the cost savings found in recycling case folders. Like an office manager on steroids, this personality busily works at forming new committees, rewriting hiring policies, penciling budgets and relocating water coolers.

At first, it seems that this type of managing partner is taking control by managing the details of the firm's operation. Everyone seems relieved. The firm soon realizes, however, that the changes being made are superficial and, in some cases, downright childish.

This type of managing partner applies Band-Aids to the outer shell of a firm. Unfortunately, lasting and fundamental change cannot be achieved in this way. It must start within the core and move outward. Trying to get to the core from the outside is like drilling for water in the desert. You won't find any.

The Workhorse

Just because a partner generates high levels of billing revenue and has a strong work ethic does not automatically mean he has the requisite skills and expertise to effectively lead and manage the firm.

If the managing partner is a "workhorse," he may expect that other members of the firm will follow his lead. Unfortunately, while leading by example is admirable, it rarely has staying power. The "be like Mike" approach may temporarily stimulate more work activity among lawyers and staff, but rarely does it result in lasting change if it is not also accompanied by strong leadership. What it often *does* cause is resentment on the part of the new managing partner as he sadly realizes that the firm's lawyers are not taking his cue—he's the only one burning the midnight oil.

Lewis, of Detroit, shared this experience:

> *I came up the ranks by tracing the footsteps of our top guy.*
> *He was always the last to leave and the first in. I thought*
> *being like him would get me to the top. It did. But when I*
> *got there, the lawyers I managed didn't care about tracing*
> *my footsteps or emulating my work ethic. Most want to know*
> *"What's in it for me?" before they break their backs.*

A managing partner should spend time managing, leading and marketing the firm, but spending more time managing and less time with clients takes an otherwise productive senior timekeeper away from generating revenue. Firms should think seriously about the consequences of this type of situation.

The Rainmaker

It is a common mistake to believe that a star rainmaker will make a star managing partner. Actually, quite the contrary is true.

There is little to support the contention that those who can make rain will also be great managers—in fact, they are typically poor managers. They can be great communicators and sometimes even great relationship builders, but they often lack the patience and discipline necessary to cope with the challenges of building and leading their firm to new heights, and it is difficult for them to lead in the face of adversity and rise above firm politics. While rainmakers understandably wield much power, the reality is that the ultimate success of a firm will depend on an entirely different type of leader with an entirely different set of skills.

Let's take an in-depth look at rainmakers since these types have traditionally dominated the legal landscape.

The Rainmaker's Legacy. Great rainmakers, known simply and affectionately as the "Great Ones," have always been valuable commodities. The question is whether or not they make great leaders and managers.

It's true that firms have often experienced great growth at the hands of great rainmakers. Almost mythical in stature, some of these mega-lawyers have single-handedly elevated their firms to great heights. In doing so, they became the heart and soul of the firm's persona.

In my discussions with lawyers about the character traits of their firms' rainmakers, a dominant character pattern emerged: Rainmakers don't delegate well. They hoard knowledge. They are highly political, stubbornly independent by nature and mavericks by impulse.

Rainmakers resemble what business thinkers call "Phase-One Entrepreneurs." These are core-level players. They get things done—often by imposing their will on others. They never say die. They are obsessive and have great tenacity; but at some point, the management and business skills necessary to take their organization to the next level are simply not compatible with this type of person's nature or desires. Ironically, the character qualities found in top rainmakers are often strikingly different from those found in top managers.

In large firms, rainmakers are famous for letting the firm's business be managed by executive committee—not because committee action is superior, but because rainmakers would rather not be bothered with such headaches. However, it is obvious that an executive committee can never replace the leadership and management strength necessary to take a firm to a higher level.

One very prominent rainmaker described his role at the firm this way: "This firm was built on my reputation, and to this day, it runs on my reputation. The single most irritating trait of my partners is when they don't want to do things my way. The main role of the managing partner is being able to keep the discontent factor of the other partners to an absolute minimum."

To most rainmakers, marketing means reeling in new clients—preferably big ones with substantial and broad-based legal needs. For firms with such a rainmaker as managing partner, the rainmaker *is* the firm's marketing. That is, until the rainmaker leaves.

When the "Great One" Leaves. When the Great One leaves, a large void is created. The Great One leaves behind not only his legacy, but also a firm without a leader. All too often the space he vacated is left unfilled by the remaining partners. The truth is, these types of powerhouse partners are hard acts to follow, and their absence can loom as large and as real as their presence once did.

Uncertainty often follows the departure of such a personality. For most partners it's a very unsettling experience. The next in line—the re-placements— often perceive their new positions after such a transition as temporary holding stations until the next best leader can be resurrected, hopefully in the image of the Great One.

Taking the helm, especially in inclement weather, has destroyed other-wise promising careers. Some newly ordained managing partners decide to just wait it out. They are managing partners by default, and their sole interest is to stay the course.

These types hedge their bets, keep an active caseload, service the big clients and, if time permits, try to manage the firm. Like good soldiers, they keep their heads down and ears open.

If trying to step into the shoes of a Great One sounds intimidating, it usually is. However take comfort in the fact that in times of transition, and in particular when the Great One leaves, everyone's expectations are depressingly low. As we shall soon see, this can be used to your advantage.

It's important to keep in mind that great personalities come and go. Values, on the other hand, have staying power, especially when they be-come a living part of the firm's culture. Once you have committed to mak-ing a change in your firm, your vision will help inspire others.

The reality is, however, that your rising to the challenge does not guar-antee that every member of the firm will do the same. Some seem to de-rive more satisfaction from being entrenched and stagnant than from cul-tivating change and growth.

The Best Type of Managing Partner

The best type of managing partner is the one most committed to lead. But leadership is not a singular activity; it is a reciprocal process. Other partners and associates must be prepared to support and follow the lead of this partner. In most cases, this means that they must have a willingness to be managed.

Ken Stuart, a partner in a large Bay Area firm, shared the following:

> *Our firm has over a hundred and fifty partners. What's missing among this diverse group is a shared sense of purpose— a shared sense of vision and respect for what each of us, as partners, contributes to the firm. Instead, more often than not, we're a fragmented bunch. Most of us don't even have a clue what the other practice groups are doing.*
>
> *I see the problem as twofold. First, partners are not willing to be managed; this is huge barrier for us. We are all marching to a different drummer. Second—and this is probably a result of our first problem—each partner feels that what he does as a partner is more valuable to the firm than what other partners do.*
>
> *Our rainmakers believe that the other partners should be more like them—always working on bringing in new clients. Other partners see it differently.*

In truth, it is common for partners to believe that if all the rest of the partners were only like them, the rest of the firm's issues would fall nicely into place. It's the nature of the human ego. But this is where true leadership comes in. When a leader emerges whom everyone in the firm respects, this person will be able to convince the others to follow his vision. And a truly intelligent leader, as we will soon see, has a vision that incorporates everyone's dream.

Beware of Toxic Partners (Toxics)

It's been said that one bad apple can ruin the entire barrel. Such sayings have withstood the test of time precisely because they contain more than just a grain of truth.

Often a firm's inability or unwillingness to change can be traced to one individual, one obstinate personality—usually an equity partner—whom I call the "Toxic Partner."

By Toxic Partner, I don't mean just the ordinary troublemaker—the person who lacks a sense of humor or is emotionally stilted. I am speaking of the partner who is beyond being difficult and obnoxious—the one who is downright lethal to your mental health and that of your firm.

Toxics kill off possibility just by being presented to it. No matter what the idea is, Toxics find and dwell on the negative. They thrive on it. Toxics despise teamwork and promote the worst forms of cynicism. They hate smiles and delight in frowns. They are often arrogant, selfish and overbearing.

The behavior of toxics can take many forms. Often they assume a *superior position*, insisting on imposing their supposed *higher standards* on others at the expense of the firm. They live in their own emotionally twisted box, unable to see the good in anyone or anything. They're a drain on life itself.

Toxics are chronic complainers. They breed dissatisfaction. They take pleasure in dwelling in an emotional abyss and love to cause dissension throughout the ranks. They thrive on telling people things can't be done, and you can rely on them to be the first to say, "I told you so!" when you falter.

Having a Toxic on your team is like having your very own firm Antichrist. For the Toxic, sadly, there can be no redemption. You may think you can rescue someone from his own drowning, but chances are you will end up drowning yourself and the entire firm in the process.

Maybe you have a Toxic sharing your firm's power base. Maybe it's someone you've known for years. Perhaps you even made partner together and, over the years, you've developed a bond with this person. Am I suggesting you turn your back on him and walk him to the door?

That is exactly what I am suggesting. If possible, strap him to a dolly and speed-roll him out the back door. Nothing short of full and complete ejection will do. It will require damage control, yes, but the alternative—doing nothing—is far worse than you can imagine. Don't wait for the problems to multiply, because they will, and often by the time the rest are willing take action, it will be too late.

Science has demonstrated that emotional states in organizations are viral in nature. The reason for this is that less dominant personalities tend to get absorbed by the emotions and moods of others with whom they work. Like the chameleon that changes colors to fit the situation, Toxics change their stories to fit the circumstances, making it appear that they are victims in an attempt to cover the fact that they are the real source of the firm's misery. Keep in mind, however, that the misery is almost always of their own making.

Toxicity at the power-sharing level has a way of rippling down by emotional osmosis. If there is a Toxic, there is usually only one, but he will have his own sphere of influence, sometimes surrounded by others who are guilty of negativity more by association than by any significant toxicity on their own part. They are mostly followers and pose no real threat to the firm's stability. When the Toxic has been removed, there will be no center of gravity—nothing to revolve around—and those who had surrounded him will scatter away in confusion.

The challenge, of course, is how to rid a firm of its Toxic Partner. In a midsize Chicago firm, the first plan was to hope the Toxic would leave on his own. One of the firm's main partners told me:

> *Everyone knows the partner who has been holding us back—it's no secret. It's painfully obvious. But it's also naïve to suggest that, once we confront this person, he will just pick up and leave. He is entrenched here. If he leaves, it's quite likely that some of our important clients will leave also. Maybe he'll*

*take some of our lawyers as well. And that's not considering
the lawsuits that will likely follow. It's a can of worms no one
here is prepared to open.*

Not opening the proverbial can of worms offers a false sense of security. By not opening the can, one thing is certain: You'll never get the Toxic
in one, where he belongs. Instead he'll stay, having his way as usual, stunt-
ing growth and strangling every bit of vitality out of the firm. Remember,
keeping the status quo is only an illusion. If you're not moving forward,
you're moving backward.

So, if you are committed to lead, your very first challenge is to deal with
the reality of getting rid of your Toxic, if there is one, as soon as possible.
Powerful leaders never waste time when forced to make difficult choices.

Nothing will be accomplished by closing your eyes to the problem. It's
time to close ranks and expose the Toxic once and for all. Rendering the
Toxic's actions visible can cause him to quickly lose power. But nothing
will happen until you take the bull by the horns and finally wrestle him
to the ground. Often what's needed is the oldest tactic of all—threatening
with one hand while holding out the olive branch with the other. Do whatever is needed—just don't let fear stop you.

Trying to appease a Toxic almost never works. It is practically impossible to reform a Toxic, and trying to will only worsen the situation. Instead,
along with your inner team, you must deal with this issue directly and rid
yourselves of the Toxic once and for all. If handled correctly, more often
than not the Toxic will leave. When the Toxic is exposed for who he is, it
will become intolerable for him to stay.

Once your decision is made, the last thing you want is to take half measures with this kind of person. When he is exposed, the Toxic will use his
tricks to undermine you. He will work underground to destroy you and
all who oppose him—even if it means bringing down the rest of the firm.
Your goal should be to deprive him of this opportunity as fast as you can.

Toxics rarely, if ever, change. This is unfortunate, but you must consider
the larger picture: Either you let one person hold back an entire firm—and

he will—or you make the very difficult and painful choice of ousting him. Leaders do not bury their heads in the sand. They see reality as it is and take the necessary action toward resolution.

Sometimes we give Toxics too much credit. Often they are more bark than bite. We see them as powerful, but the strength they project is often just an expression of their own fear and weakness. Their misery is usually deeply rooted in their own sense of inadequacy. There is no easy solution for these types of people. You do not have the expertise or the time to figure out what specific pathology has invaded this poor person's psyche, but know this: It will take much more than twelve sessions of therapy and a "primal scream" to bring him back. So stop playing God and get on with transforming your firm.

Getting rid of Toxics in this way smacks of Machiavellian tactics—but dealing with such people requires nothing less. Desperate situations call for desperate measures. There is never anything to be gained by allowing one person to bring down an entire enterprise.

The Big Decision

If you're the person chosen to lead your firm's reinvention, before you expend the energy this will require, ask yourself a big question: *Is this the right firm for me?* Only you know the answer. Maybe it is and you can find a way of removing the Toxic. That's a viable possibility—and it's strongly recommended if you think the firm has great potential. But do not delude yourself. If you're not up to the challenge, don't do it. You won't be the first lawyer to pick up and leave, and you won't be the last.

If you choose to take the challenge, find the courage to make tough decisions and choose an excellent team to help you lead the firm through its reinvention. Otherwise tomorrow will be like every other day—more of the same, month after month, year after year. Remember, no one ever does great things by playing small. So make a decision and make it happen.

Finding Your Firm's Vision

In the initial meetings of your inner circle, before you start describing the firm's vision, the group must first determine whether the law your firm practices and the clients it serves are compatible with its real interests and values. Wanting to change practice areas is not unusual among law firms, and changing them is not as big an obstacle as you might think. Many firms choose to find new practice areas and new types of clients that actually inspire them while slowly phasing out those that don't. Changing what you do and whom you do it for may seem like unrealistic luxuries, but if you are committed to transforming your firm to the highest level possible, the initial meetings of the inner circle are the place to address these very fundamental issues.

Some firms acknowledge that their existing base of clients is too valuable to phase out, so they keep that client base while developing new practice areas that are more consistent with their interests and values. The members of the inner circle must be brutally honest with themselves about whether something like this could work for them. Otherwise, why spend the time, money and emotional investment of redefining your firm only to recognize that you're still working in the wrong area and serving the wrong people?

One San Diego family lawyer expressed it like this:

> *I've been practicing family law for over twenty years. I can't tell you how much I dislike family law. Divorce brings out the worst in people. Most of my clients become miserable and vindictive. You never hear a positive word out of their mouths. All I do is fight the traffic to get to court to argue motions that, quite frankly, are ridiculous. I was at a crossroads when I finally decided to move into a practice area that I found much more interesting and satisfying. I'm doing estate planning now. While I still have my share of family law clients, I no longer feel chained to them. I have found a niche that really works for me, and my billings are still where I need them to be.*

For now, let's assume that the inner circle has decided that your firm is already working in its chosen area of law. The next order of business is to begin the process of reinventing your firm from the inside out.

Learning how to shape your firm to its fullest potential is no easy task. It takes both commitment and leadership. To take this journey, you must first have a road map that will take you step by step. Don't even think about cutting corners. Every step must be completed, as it will lay the foundation for the next.

This reshaping process has worked for others, and if you are committed to it, it will work for you. First, you need to identify the specific *challenges* facing your firm. They may not be obvious at first. Challenges are areas in which you really want to see constructive and measurable qualitative change. They can be in the areas of service, revenue building, morale, quality and quantity of work product, or profit levels per partner—the list is yours for the making.

Where Is Your Firm Now?

Finding your firm's challenges requires an honest assessment of your firm's current state, and it is a time to have your eyes wide open.

You may be feeling vitalized at this point—eager to get started rebuilding your firm. If so, take a deep breath and consider this statement:

> *You* cannot *begin the rebuilding process without first examining your existing challenges and problem areas.*

Some of you will respond by asking, "What's to examine? *Everything* here needs changing." Perhaps, but to get where you want to go, you first need to really understand where you've been. This means taking a hard and honest look at your existing firm. Most lawyers are inclined to skip this process. They would rather not open up old wounds, and looking in the mirror can be painful. So they take the path of least resistance instead: They try to write a great-sounding firm mission statement and hope that it reflects what they really want to accomplish.

This type of reasoning will sink the ship before it ever sets sail. The process does not work this way! It's like trying to change your hairstyle without the benefit of a mirror—or worse, like taking on a new client without ever having met or communicated with her! (Remember how many times you have told new clients that you need to know *everything*, both the good parts and the bad!)

You can't possibly know what you want without also looking at what you *don't* want. They are opposite sides of the same coin. The benefit of such an examination of the firm lies in discovering what you weren't aware of before.

Challenges?

If you can't think of any major challenges facing your firm, answering the questions in Figure 9.1 will bring them bubbling up. Notice how many of the challenges addressed are multidimensional and can apply to more than one aspect of the firm.

FIGURE 9.1: Identifying Your Firm's Challenges

FIRM CULTURE

How would you describe your firm's culture?

How is your firm perceived by your associates?

How is your firm perceived by your partners?

What does the firm's physical presence communicate?

Is firm management committed to the growth and development of its people?

Is there complacency among your lawyers?

Is there complacency among your staff and administration?

Does your firm tolerate politics?

How does your firm handle gossip?

Do you encourage team performance rather than individual competitiveness?

FIRM PERFORMANCE

How is the firm perceived by your competition?

What is your firm best known for in your legal community?

Is your firm's compensation system tied to performance?

How do you define attorney performance?

What percentage of your lawyers know the firm's goals?

What is your firm's policy toward growth?

How many hours per week do your associates devote to business development?

In what ways is your firm innovative?

How would you rate your firm's technological competence?

Do associates push themselves to learn new skills?

Do partners push themselves to improve their management skills?

How does the firm encourage teams versus individual performance?

How does leadership reward the firm's support staff for quality performance?

CLIENT SERVICE

How is your firm perceived by your clients?

How do you measure client satisfaction?

What are your firm's top three inspired values in client service?

How responsive is your staff to clients' needs?

Are you meeting or exceeding your clients' expectations?

What is your firm's definition of service?

What can your clients count on when they do business with your firm?

Do your clients rave about the quality of your service?

What percentage of new business is from existing clients?

ADMINISTRATIVE AND SUPPORT SYSTEMS

What is your firm's policy toward recruiting talent?

Do you offer your lawyers and staff development training?

What is your secretarial staff accountable for?

Do your associates and staff perceive the firm as fair?

In what ways are you supportive of your attorneys?

In what ways are you supportive of your staff?

Do you encourage your lawyers and staff to stretch their skills?

DEDICATION AND LEADERSHIP

Do you offer lawyers effective leadership training?

Do you encourage lawyers and staff to be independent thinkers?

Are you committed to mentoring associates?

Do the lawyers and staff feel they have a future at your firm?

Do your associates genuinely aspire to become partners?

Do you regularly provide constructive review and performance tips?

Does your firm work as a team?

Discovering the Big Challenges: Going to the Source

In my work with firms, I ask partners to identify the areas they believe will be the most difficult to change—problems they consider insurmountable. Although sometimes it takes a little prodding, eventually the partners reveal not mere challenges, but areas of deep concern that they have given up on. Not surprisingly, these challenges are frequently the very issues that mean the most to the partners, and not being able to achieve them is often the source of their deepest frustration and cynicism.

Ironically, I find that most partners, once they are able to identify and confront what they believe to be unchangeable problems, also realize how much their cynicism has prevented them from solving these problems. After honest discussions, most are willing to take on these "insurmountable" challenges rather than sweep them back under the rug. In doing so, they acquire a renewed sense of urgency—a need to break through old barriers and bury their demons once and for all. Indeed, acknowledging the problems means that they have won their first big battle.

Bringing big challenges to the surface brings partners together and puts them back into the game of reinventing their firms.

Finding More Challenges: Speaking with Your Clients

Another way to find more of your firm's challenges is to speak with your clients—the people who actually use your services. While this must be done skillfully, and must be done by the most senior partners—not by administrative or marketing staff—it can be the most productive path to finding new ways of serving your clients.

In fact, some of the most successful firms make such client meetings mandatory at the conclusion of an engagement with a client. After a case ends, the most senior partner in the group meets with the client and discusses the firm's performance. The goal of this discussion is to discover ways in which the firm can provide continually higher levels of service.

These "completion meetings" must be done with the right intentions. Just coming in and asking if there were any problems can alienate the client. The partner holding the meeting is there to learn about the client's experiences during the engagement. The goal is to bring added value to the relationship.

The challenge of this type of meeting, if you are the person holding it, is to be able to hear clients' concerns without letting your own personality and feelings get in the way. Not all clients will open up. They must first believe that your intentions are genuine and not part of a strategy to generate additional business for the firm.

To make it easy for your client to speak candidly, *you* must speak candidly. Explain to clients that finding out more about how the engagement went from their perspective is essential to being able to offer more useful ways of serving them. They will appreciate your time, and your interest in their opinions will demonstrate the firm's integrity and commitment to service. Doing this will also allow you to tie up loose ends and make sure you complete the engagement on a positive note.

During this meeting, acknowledge clients for putting their trust in you and your firm, and make sure that nothing was left undone. Specifically ask whether the firm kept the client informed and was accessible and responsive. Then widen the scope and find out as much as possible about what worked for clients and what didn't. Keeping the discussion open-ended will encourage your client to express a full range of issues, some of which might not otherwise be explored.

Being successful at holding completion meetings is an art form that separates true professionals from the rest. Unlike the initial meetings leading up to your first engagement with the client, completion meetings will add immediate value to your relationship and provide critical insight for your firm.

A few tips for success at completion meetings are worth mentioning:

- Never use a completion meeting as an occasion for soliciting additional business from the client. This will appear manipulative and insincere.

- Never become defensive or attempt to explain problems away. It is the client's experiences that matter here. Remember, you asked for the meeting.

- If things need to be made right, make them right without making the client wrong. The goal is to listen, not to judge.

- Allocate adequate time for the meeting and remember to turn off your cell phone or pager. Make sure the client is not billed for the meeting.

- Don't be put off if clients are initially suspicious or surprised by your questions. At first, they might be reluctant to tell you what they really think. Be persistent and, above all, be honest with them. Tell them that your firm is committed to providing a higher level of service to its clients and, to that end, you are seeking their honest and candid input.

- Lead with a simple question: "What service could we provide that would make our firm really extraordinary in your eyes?" Most clients will start giving you clues. Keep listening and keep asking questions; their insights will almost always enlighten you.

The Four-Step Inquiry

Once you have identified the major challenges facing your firm and have fully articulated them in writing, the next job is to prioritize them. One firm I worked with came up with more than fifty challenges before refining the list to those that were the most compelling!

One way of prioritizing your challenges is to perform a four-step inquiry for each one. This process will help you to identify areas that need immediate work and attention, but more importantly, the inquiry will lay the groundwork for developing your firm's charter, and in the end, will shape your firm's unique brand of service.

For each of your major challenges, ask the following questions:

1.   *What's absent?*

2.   *What if what is absent were present?*
     How would this change things?

3.   *What types of inspired values drive this type of change?*

4.   *What specific actions come from such inspired values?*

Examples of the Four-Step Inquiry
The first step is to look at what's absent in the challenged area, the presence of which, if it were there, would profoundly and positively change this area for the better. From this you can identify what specific values drive such a change. Finding your inspired values is like finding precious stones. Values once discovered form the basis on which the firm's actions can later be measured. Moreover, inspired values like these, because they embody truth, have the potential to motivate and inspire in powerful ways.

Let's look at two examples of how the four-step inquiry works.

EXAMPLE 1

Describe the challenge: We need to treat our clients better, especially when they visit our office. How we receive clients is so ordinary. Clients sit down and wait for the lawyer to pick them up from the reception area. They read through boring magazines. Maybe they get a cup of watered-down coffee while they wait. Lawyers and staff walk past them and don't even acknowledge their presence. The atmosphere is sterile and artificial and impersonal.

1. What's absent? The clients' experience of feeling genuinely welcomed and respected at the firm.

2. What if what is absent were present? How would this change things? Clients would view the firm in a more positive light. Associates would begin to develop a personal sensitivity toward the firm's clients. This would be uplifting for the clients as well as for the firm.

3. What types of inspired values drive this type of change? Honoring clients as guests. Caring for their comfort. Respecting their presence.

4. What specific actions come from such inspired values? Every guest is greeted respectfully and cordially. The reception area is filled with clippings of the firm's major clients and their accomplishments, including stories about how the firm was able to help clients reach their goals. The reception area includes a copy of the firm's charter, listing the firm's goals and its commitments to clients. The firm encourages a culture that makes lawyers and staff feel comfortable acknowledging guests. The firm offers its clients quality beverages in interesting serving cups.

If this example rings true to you—if it inspires you—then you have just hit upon some inspired values that have the power to transform your firm. In fact, they might be the beginning of your firm's charter and might sound like this: "We *respect, care* about and *honor* our clients..." What makes these words so powerful is that they are backed by *your* inspired values and are translated into your firm's behavior, which demonstrates *your* commitment in real and tangible terms. This is what firm character building is all about. It's the true measure of a firm being what it says it is.

Let's consider another example.

EXAMPLE 2

Describe the challenge: Associates need to work at higher levels and take on more responsibility. Most are not motivated. They seem to work hard, but they don't go the extra distance. They rarely show personal initiative. They don't seem to be team players. Their goal is to bill two hundred hours and go home. They have the type of paycheck mentality that produces mediocre work. The partners don't really know much about them outside of their work product.

1. What's absent? Associates feeling that they share in the firm's future. Associates seeing their role as part of a larger team effort. Partners being committed to management and leading.

2. What if what is absent were present? How would this change things? Associates would know in a tangible way that the firm's success is tied directly to their own personal and professional goals. Associates would have pride in their work product and know that the quality of their colleagues' work actually impacts them.

3. What types of inspired values drive this type of change? Commitment to associates' professional and personal development. A shared purpose in which the success of the firm is directly tied to the success of the associates. Trust and respect for associates so that they will respond in kind to new levels of opportunity and growth.

4. What specific actions come from such inspired values? Partners and management are given time to get to know the associates and learn about their personal and professional goals. Management communicates clearly to associates about how reaching the firm's goals will also result in the associates reaching their own goals. Promotions and compensation are tied to performance and firm contribution as well as to team performance levels. A strong mentoring system, designed to prepare associates for assuming greater levels of responsibility commensurate with tangible financial incentives, is instituted. A firm-wide policy of ze-ro-tolerance for gossip and firm politics is established.

Facilitating the Four-Step Process

The firm can facilitate the four-step process on its own or bring in an expert. The idea of hiring an outside expert is new to law firms, and most partners feel uncomfortable with the prospect. Nevertheless, use of an outside expert is highly recommended.

In the business world, it's quite common to use experts to facilitate operational change and find new ways of managing objectives. Such people, if they have the proper skills, can be of tremendous value in holding up a mirror to the firm while maintaining the perspective and objectivity the process requires.

It is highly advantageous to use a facilitator who is also a lawyer with management and operational experience—first, because such a facilitator will be able to learn about and understand your firm quickly, and second, because the partners will feel confident and comfortable in the knowledge that the facilitator has personally experienced the unique demands of the practice and management side of law.

The disadvantage of trying to bring in an outside facilitator is that it may be difficult to find one. Organizational experts who understand the unique dynamics of the legal profession, especially in the context of practice development, are rare. Most business consultants are used to working with business executives—not with a roomful of law partners.

Facilitating the process in-house is very difficult and is not recommended, because the process of looking at the overall picture while being part of it can be mind-boggling. It can seem as if there are more questions than answers. The truth is, the people involved are too close to be completely objective. This is why lawyers don't represent themselves in court and why doctors don't operate on family members—the emotions are too powerful and there's too much risk of losing your cool in such situations.

When the firm attempts to address the problems on its own, it's easy to get trapped in trying to solve the problem in the same old ways that have prevented effecting meaningful change in the past. The goal is to break away from the past and the old ways of thinking about your firm.

A skilled and experienced facilitator can help you reach this goal most effectively.

Drafting Your Master Charter

Some people call it a *mission statement*, but I prefer to use the term *charter*. *Charter* suggests a detailed approach. It implies a *process* rather than a pronouncement and seems to describe something that's more methodical than rhetorical. A charter not only defines the firm's vision and values, as a mission statement does, but also describes how the firm will achieve their goals. A charter, more so than a mission statement, calls upon your firm's inner circle to remain focused as it steers the firm toward its goals.

A mission statement, however, may be used as a stepping-stone on the way to the creation of a charter. Used in that way, it can be an essential element in the process of defining the firm. Its brevity is both a strength and a limitation—a strength in that it provides a succinct, broad, inspiring summary of the firm's commitment; a limitation in that it is too brief to offer guidance on how to fulfill that commitment.

Consider the commitments evidenced in these mission statements:

We are committed to being a world-class law firm. We help our clients navigate complex legal, financial and regulatory barriers. We value integrity, leadership and teamwork. Our methods and practices are grounded in accountability, openness and innovation.

• • •

We provide quality legal services that contribute to the success of our clients by offering informed and intelligent counsel backed by our commitment to be our best at every stage in the representation of our clients.

• • •

We are completely accountable to our clients. We are committed to our clients' growth—no matter where they are in their evolution or what their objectives might be. Whether our clients are buying, selling, acquiring or being acquired, we will always be there to serve them with our commitment to be our best.

Each pronouncement is a powerful statement. But without a process for keeping the inspired values and goals alive and relevant, they will fade into the firm's collective unconscious.

The Power of Language

Special attention must be given to drafting your firm's charter. It must be carefully structured to reflect the reality the inner circle wishes to create. The written word, when used masterfully, can evoke strong emotional responses.

Thanks to modern psycholinguistics, we are beginning to understand the ways in which language influences us. Words can trigger vivid emotions and images in the brain. Words can motivate us to take action and help us to feel a shared sense of purpose. This is especially true when such words evoke in us what we feel to be true and right.

Your firm's charter can be the vehicle for that power if it expresses the inspired values (such as integrity and honesty) of the firm's leadership. It must express what the firm values most about its practice: its commitment to its clients and the promises it will keep.

The charter must make the firm's intentions real and embody the firm's vision of the future like colors painted on canvas. This vision must inspire people to take action toward its fulfillment.

The condition precedent to the creation of any value-driven vision must be *inspiration*. Inspiration is felt at a visceral level, and it can't be faked. It moves the listener and invites actions that will fulfill the vision.

A bold vision that sounds good on paper may fail to evoke emotion. If it does not ring true, it must be discarded. Don't be seduced by clever tag lines. The single most important issue is whether the vision inspires your core leadership.

As you, the core leadership, begin to draft the firm's charter, do not be concerned about whether it will inspire others outside your group. We will get to that next. A charter that fails to inspire the core leadership will also fail to inspire others. And the converse stands—if the charter *does* inspire the inner circle, it will be likely to inspire others—those who want to share the vision. Those in your firm who are inspired will be energized and will feel that they have found a home—a place to spend their future.

Once the inner circle presents the firm's new vision, it will be easy to identify employees who either don't share the vision or are not open to it—they will be negative about the charter, and chances are they will not have to be encouraged to leave the firm. People who don't fit at a fundamental level tend to move on, and in the long run, this is to the benefit of both firm and employee. Don't be discouraged—it is said that pruning actually makes the tree grow stronger.

Your Charter

There are many ways to write a charter. It's a process that requires looking inward at what you know while looking outward—with your imagination— at what your firm might become.

Here is one approach that works well:

> Imagine that your firm, after careful consideration, has been selected by the state bar to accept its highest and most prestigious honor: recognition as the most successful law firm in the state. The honor will be presented to your core leadership by the state bar president at the annual meeting, which will be attended not only by hundreds of your colleagues, but also by recognized leaders in government and education. The president of the bar will have five minutes to articulate why your firm has been selected by your peers to receive this great honor. The tribute will leave no doubt as to why your firm is so admired and successful.
>
> *Here's the challenging part*: Your inner circle will be drafting the five-minute tribute.

Take your time and consider the words you will choose in describing your firm. What inspired values will you choose to emphasize? What does your firm stand for? What is your firm committed to? Why, among all the hundreds of firms that were considered for this honor, was your firm chosen?

The Jefferson Test

Thomas Jefferson once said that when making important decisions, he tried to imagine that all the people he most admired and respected were in the room with him, watching and listening to what he said and did.

Your core leadership should think about Jefferson's technique as it chooses inspired values to guide the firm's future. Will these values hold up to the scrutiny of people you admire and respect? If those people were in the room watching you debate the relative worth of your firm's inspired values, would they be pleased by your choices, or would they think you were not reaching high enough?

Your charter must embody the purpose and inspired values of the firm. It must envision the future—what the firm *will be*—as a standard against which everything else can be measured. It will be the set of fundamental principles by which the firm will operate.

A charter begins with a declaration of clear intention—a statement of identity that elicits both a picture of and a feeling about what the firm stands for. It is a guide, explaining how people within the organization will serve its purpose.

The charter is also a collective commitment that everything the firm does will be done in a certain way. It must articulate what clients and others can expect from the firm. Most importantly, it must make clear the firm's commitment to be accountable at every level, from the senior partner to the receptionist at the front desk.

Drafting your firm's charter is no simple task. It will require imagining and thinking in ways that are not restricted by the firm's past, but that allow the inner circle to envision what is possible for the firm's future. An effective charter, authentically developed, can encourage momentum in the firm's reinvention process—especially in times of uncertainty.

The Defining Process

Once the core leadership has identified the firm's inspired values, the next step is to integrate them into a powerful statement of intent—the firm's master charter. This process and the process that naturally follows will be the wind that pushes the sails of your vision forward.

People can forget the spoken word, and often do, but the written word has staying power and can be communicated and referenced over and over again. Think of the United States Constitution. The power of its language comes from its clarity of purpose. It sets out a *vision* (where we are going), an *organizing structure* (how it will work), and *values and principles* (why we are doing what we are doing).

Developing a charter is vital to the firm's enterprise. It is the organizing principle around which the firm's purpose can be communicated and its actions measured.

Every partner and primary administrator must participate in some meaningful way in the creation of the firm's charter, because the creative process is just as important as the final document.

One of the most significant aspects of my work with firms is to assist them in developing their firm's master charter, after which we work on *derivative charters* for every department and practice group in the organization. It is the process of defining and redefining what we do and what we are accountable for that drives the power of clarity into every corner of the organization.

The major components of the charter-creation process are defined below and displayed in Figure 10.1.

Master Charter: The master charter is drafted by the core leadership (inner circle) of the firm. It must clearly articulate the basic purpose of the firm, including the firm's deepest convictions and values.

FIGURE 10.1: The Charter Structure

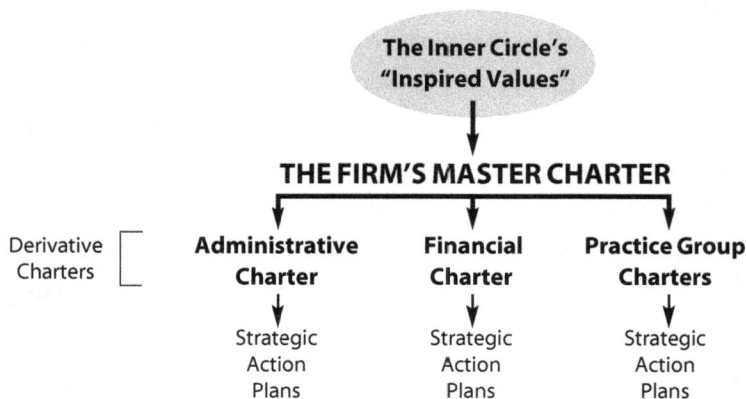

152

Derivative Charters: Derivative charters are crafted by the major organizational units of the firm—the executive committee as well as the other major functional units and groups of the firm. Each unit must define and make clear its own functional purpose, values and aims within the specific context of fulfilling the broader purpose declared in the master charter.

Strategic Action Plans: Strategic action plans are drafted by the major organizational units of the firm and are task-specific with respect to purpose, time and responsibility. These plans must be consistent with both the derivative charters and the master charter.

Begin with the Envisioned Charter, Then Work Backward

Finding a vision and getting key people on board is the firm's first major hurdle in the reinvention process. The second is implementation. Building a bridge to the firm's future requires both imagination and creativity—the ability to see the firm as a complete expression of the charter's fulfillment.

Over thirty years ago, Tom Watson, the founder of perhaps the greatest service company ever built—IBM—was asked what he attributed the company's incredible success to. His response is relevant to our discussion of how vision can translate into form.

> *I started with a very clear picture of what I thought was the ideal service company. I wanted to see in my mind what it would look like once it was done—once the vision of what was in my mind was in place. I then imagined how such a company would have to act to be that way. From this I created a picture of how IBM would have to act when it was finally done.*
>
> *What I realized was that if I was ever to get our new company to be and look a certain way, we would have to start acting that way right now and keep on acting that way.*

I realized that for IBM to become a great company, it would have to act like a great company long before it ever became one. From the outset, IBM was fashioned after my vision. At the end of each day, we asked ourselves how well we had done, discovered the disparity between where we were and where we had committed ourselves to be, and at the start of the following day, set out to make up for the difference.

By focusing on the completed picture, the inner circle will begin to visualize which systems and processes are necessary to fulfill its vision. This requires stepping back and connecting the dots. The more dots you connect, the more you can see of the whole picture. Knowing how to think creatively really pays off during this process.

Bridging the Gaps with Strategic Action Plans

Strategic action plans are specific, goal-oriented road maps that exist for the sole purpose of turning the firm's charter into a tangible reality. They act as bridges. If the charter is the brain, these plans are the muscle and nervous systems that channel the aims described by the charter into specific, measurable action.

Strategic action plans are developed only *after* the firm's master charter has been carved out by its core leadership and derivative charters have been developed by the firm's departments. The master charter and derivative charters are the foundation on which strategic decisions and actions are made.

Well-thought-out strategic action plans—when they are logical extensions of the firm's values and beliefs—are naturally imbued with the firm's culture. They can take on enormous momentum that will be capable of pushing the firm forward to new heights and performance levels.

Moreover, when the firm's culture embraces the inspired norms and values of the charter, those norms and values actually make people in the firm reject individual or group conduct that is inconsistent with the charter. Like a bad germ, such conduct is sweated out—it's simply not tolerated. People will recognize such conduct and will not be shy about pointing it out and saying, "Sorry, but that's simply not how things are done around here." Strategic action plans map the course by which the firm's leadership develops. The leaders then manage the necessary talent and resources to achieve the firm's broader goals.

Putting It All Together

The ultimate goal of writing a charter is to carve your beautiful elephant—your reinvented firm—out of your block of marble. Ideally, the result of this process will be a firm-wide map headed by the master charter, with every derivative charter articulated and supported by clear and concise strategic action plans that include time lines and performance measures.

As members of the firm examine the big picture described by the master charter, derivative charters and strategic action plans, they will realize— perhaps for the first time—where the firm is going and how and when it will get there. From this point on, the process is really about connecting the dots and making sure everything gets done.

Since the derivative charters are expressed in terms of the master charter and measured against it, there will finally be a tangible way to ensure that the goals of the firm and the goals of its parts are in alignment. If the inner circle has done its job well, there will be a new sense of clarity and purpose upon which everyone can be measured—and since the work is relevant to each member of the firm, the majority of them will climb on board.

Once your charter is implemented, who you say you are will ring true. The firm may need to fine-tune parts of its image, but this is a function of grooming what the firm is rather than the firm wishing to be something it is not.

Many big firms want to see results of their charter-creation process immediately. With the power of today's technology and communications, integration of the firm's parts can happen faster than ever before. E-mail lists can correspond to goals and departments—communications can be brought to a whole new level. Despite this, firm-wide transformation *will* take time. I believe that a time line of two to three years is very realistic, though people will start to see many benefits in a matter of months as the firm begins to experience greater levels of clarity and alignment of firm-wide purpose, especially when the firm begins to experience the power of teamwork.

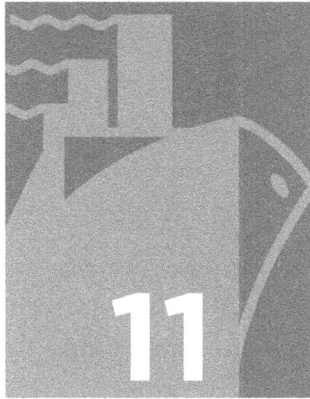

Bringing the Rest on Board

Your firm's charter is complete. You have found your vision. You feel inspired. Now it's just a matter of bringing the rest of the firm on board. You decide to have a few of those "Come to Jesus" meetings and then follow them up with a few strong memos from key partners. Soon enough, your firm's transformation will be accomplished, right? Think again. The firm is out to change its culture and its belief structure. This is not an easy task. Jack Provost describes what happened when management at his firm wrote a new mission statement but, unfortunately, stopped there:

> *Last year, my partners and I put together our firm's mission statement. It really helped us focus on what was important about our firm. It was a real accomplishment. When it was done, we sent it around the firm for feedback. People thought it was really a good idea. I even had our firm newsletter re-designed so that our mission statement could be prominently featured.*

While it did get us more focused and added some vitality, in a few months that familiar indifference returned. I guess you can't expect much from these types of things...

In order for change to take place, the firm's vision must be extended outward from the core leadership. It must reach every lawyer and staff member in your firm. Firm members must see *themselves* as constituting the vision. The firm's future must include them, both personally and professionally. Achieving the firm's vision must become a collective process.

This means that the firm must have an active and fully engaged management; a coalition of determined and powerful partners and staff is needed to see this process through. Anything less will cause confusion and cynicism throughout the firm.

A Great Master Charter Can Provide a False Sense of Security
Accomplishing the first steps toward change—working through the value defining process and writing the firm's master charter—can lead to a false sense of security. At this point, it's easy for the partners to believe that the power of the statement will itself be sufficient to carry out the plan—as if words alone contain the necessary instructions and encouragement to construct a new culture. *The charter alone will not do that, and any such expectation on the part of the core leadership will soon turn into widespread disappointment.*

This does not mean that drafting your master charter is not absolutely necessary—it is vital. Indeed, the master charter is the foundation from which everything else will follow. But do not make the mistake of stopping the *defining process* with the creation of the charter.

Alone, your firm's charter may be inspiring, but its vision will die without a sustained commitment to keep it alive. The firm's master charter is but one sweeping stroke against the backdrop of the canvas called your firm. Keep in mind that it is not the end of the defining process but rather the beginning.

The next step is for each of the firm's major departments, practice groups and committees to integrate and make relevant the principles and promises of the master charter by drafting their own derivative charters.

A master charter is like the architect's first rendering of his vision. A vision may inspire and even call others into action, but it won't tell them how and what to do to build the structure. For that, "plans" are required. For our purposes, the plans include both the firm's derivative charters and their respective strategic action plans.

Derivative Charters

Even the most spirited, well-meaning charters will fade without specific plans and processes around which the structure of the organization is built. Building such plans is best left to the specific groups and departments that are accountable for their success. Whether it's the firm's accounting department, human resources department, client services department or key practice groups, each must develop a derivative charter, the express purpose of which is the fulfillment of the firm's master charter.

The process of defining the firm must include the firm at large—at every level, in every department and practice group. Each of these groups must be part of the creative and interpretive process—and each must be made accountable for the successful integration of the group's own goals with the firm's master principles and goals.

How Change *Doesn't* Happen

Fundamental change must originate from the core leadership's inspired values. It requires the active and intense engagement of the firm's partners and key administrators. Handing out books like *Who Moved My Cheese?* for discussion in management meetings may lift a few eyebrows, but it won't facilitate change.

Nor will spouting traditional marketing theories:

> *Provide quality work and outstanding service to clients.*

Think and act like a team.

Demand integrity.

Above all, listen to your clients.

Although most firms would say that they deeply believe in these values, they haven't a clue about how to implement them. In fact, few firms even try—ironically, they're simply too busy managing the business day to day to make time for such additional work.

From Theory to Practice

The dilemma is that, even though most firms clearly understand the importance of instilling good business values, they have not been able to figure out meaningful ways to translate theory into practice.

Some try to motivate their employees by modifying their policy manuals to include the firm's cherished values and goals. For example, they add statements of belief in the importance of "teamwork," "trust" and "being in the service" of their clients.

Some firms try to instill values solely by constructing clever incentive programs that financially reward those who demonstrate compliance with firm values. The goal of these rewards is to instill values and raise ethical standards *solely* by paying workers into compliance. Relying on compensation alone to stimulate character and ethics in people is ludicrous—and what's worse, paying for professionalism sends the wrong message to employees.

Professionalism should be something your people acquire when they are in alignment with your firm's goals—when what they are doing is an expression of your firm's unique brand of service. The firm shouldn't have to beat professionalism into its people and certainly shouldn't have to pay extra for it. Values must resonate from inside the firm. They must flow from an agreed-upon and shared point of view. Inspired values cannot be faked, mimicked or purchased.

How, then, do inspired values come into being?

They come from the firm's values and leadership. Like everything else, they begin with the creation of a shared vision that is seen as relevant to everyone in the firm.

Honoring the Process of Change

Highly successful enterprises never stop reaching for higher levels of service and performance. The same should be true for your firm, especially when your goal is to bring about a change in the firm's culture.

The process of change has no distinct beginning or end. It's about leaders building leadership skills in themselves and in those they mentor. It is not a continuing education course—it's education that keeps on continuing. This is the nature of process. As the process begins, the firm may experience resistance, but it must not allow the momentum to falter at the first sign of a problem or when someone makes a mistake.

It's wise to keep your first few initiatives a bit tempered and measured. While the core leadership will be eager to get the rest of the firm on board by working on strategic action plans, it must also consider how the rest of the firm might view its proposals. Change is a very sensitive issue, and proposing it usually tends to rock the boat a bit. So pay close attention to timing. Introducing too much too soon might alienate those the firm would like to see fully on board at the early stages of the change process.

While key players are already on board and prepared to lead the charge, the firm still needs to create momentum around the idea of change outside of this core leadership group. Remember, the rest of the firm wasn't in the conference room working through the big issues and banging out the firm's master charter. They were working at their desks and worrying about whether they still had a job.

While inspiration is unquestionably a contagious emotion and will help the core leadership in its efforts to spread the word, you will need to tread softly at the very beginning.

As the charter is presented to the rest of the firm, be sure that it is not perceived as being imposed from the outside. It *must* be seen as something that has evolved from the center of the firm's leadership. If not, many employees will view it as just another practice development strategy designed to improve the firm's bottom line—a strategy from which only the firm's partners will truly benefit.

Making the Vision Relevant to Everyone

How do you jump-start the change process? The firm's top leadership must first work to bring into the fold the less-senior lawyers and staff who make up their immediate teams. It is very important that these employees understand how their own personal and professional lives will be advanced by the changes being proposed—this is what really captures people's imagination. They must perceive that they are professionally and personally vested in the results of the change process.

It's not enough to make firm managers *feel like* they are part of the process—they must actually *be* part of the process. They must have a tangible role in the creative process, and the way to get them involved is to learn what motivates them.

Most managers honestly believe that if they do their work well, they will come to feel inspired about their work, but unfortunately, they rarely do. Instead, doing their work tends to make them feel less than complete. The reason is obvious: Managers are not living out their own vision, but rather the *firm leadership's* vision. The truth is that working to achieve another's vision is simply not as inspiring as working to achieve your own. The key, therefore, must be in helping managers, and those who work under them, to find their own vision within the context of the firm. Done well, mentoring will not only impart knowledge but also will ignite enthusiasm for the firm.

Most workers, including high-level managers, believe that it's enough to be good soldiers. But in doing so, they relinquish responsibility for creating their own personal sense of purpose—their own vision.

And without a *personal* vision and purpose, there simply cannot be passion—it's human nature. Partners do not have a monopoly on wanting their lives to be meaningful. Workers who are not emotionally and personally vested in a vision will not have a sense of purpose beyond their paycheck. So they pretend to care and appear inspired by the firm's goals, but discontent will eventually creep into their work—and with it, apathy.

All workers, whether or not they acknowledge it, want and need to fulfill their potential. It's in our genes. Our need to grow and develop is innate. Some people ignore or deny this truth. Some embrace it with all their might. In either case, the need to become more than we are now is a fundamental fact of evolution. In a sense, we would all like to one day become our own visionary—the author of our own lives.

Making the firm's vision meaningful and personal to every employee is the responsibility of members of the firm's leadership. They must make concrete efforts to learn more about people as individuals—specifically, learning about their personal and professional goals. They must understand their employees in order to show them how their personal and professional growth can be realized through the firm's growth.

One client I worked with had each of the firm's partners spend time with each of their team members individually. The team members were asked to describe the visual images they associated with personal and professional success. The process was quite mind-opening. In the beginning, most of the team members thought the exercise was kind of silly. But halfway through the process, they started to enjoy what it was uncovering. It helped them to clarify their goals and brought to the surface ways in which their individual goals could be realized through the larger goals of the firm.

If managers find that it is not possible to reconcile the goals of some employees with those of the firm—and they must be very sure of this— then there may not be enough commonality of purpose between the firm and the employee to justify keeping him or her on the payroll. Pretending there *is* a commonality of purpose only causes confusion and animosity on both sides. It is better for the human resources department to consider new ways of managing the separation process so that it is fair and constructive than to try to make the employee fit into the firm's new plan.

Unfortunately, insecurity and fear tend to dominate the process of separation. However, separation should not necessarily be perceived as a failure on anyone's part. It can simply be the result of learning people's true values and goals and finding that they are not a good fit with the values and goals of the firm.

Being able to manage the separation process intelligently and fairly is essential to the firm's credibility. This is why every major department, including human resources, must take the time and effort to develop a derivative charter. Every firm action, even termination, must acknowledge and articulate the firm's commitment to the highest level of integrity possible.

Starting the Change Process with Carefully Measured Steps
Fundamental change will not occur overnight. There is no such thing as a quick fix—especially when you're out to reshape the firm's culture and inspired values. This is why it's recommended that you begin with small, manageable, easy-to-reach goals. It's natural for people to want to see some success before jumping aboard.

The goal is to jump-start support, build momentum and establish credibility as quickly as possible. Don't get caught in the trap of being too small, too long. It can deplete the initial momentum of the process and cause it to falter and stall.

Conventional business thinking has been to take small, calculated and measured steps to effect change. I believe that this strategy works, but it works only in the beginning of the transformation process. Your firm will not be able to inch its way to success in perpetuity. This is especially true when old ways of doing things are deeply ingrained in people.

At some point—and it should be sooner rather than later—the firm's leadership will need to be make some bold moves. Otherwise, complacency will creep in and it will seem like everyone is standing around waiting for someone else to do something. This can go on for just so long—finally, rather than face the embarrassment and boredom of waiting for something really significant to happen, people will simply return to what they know—the old ways of doing things and the old ways of thinking.

Building momentum toward change can be compared to a toddler making the journey from crawling to running: first the slow crawl, then the fast one, then the baby steps—all the time falling and getting back up, driven to move faster—until all of a sudden the little tyke is running around the house, screaming for joy. You want your people to think, "Hey, we could do this! Wow, this is wild! Whoops! I fell again. Let's keep on going..."

At some point, after the firm has introduced some small changes, it must instill a sense of urgency that will mobilize employees into action. Remember, their first and most natural reaction to the changes being made is to feel threatened. They have been conditioned to fear making mistakes—to run from the prospect of failure—and doing things differently *does* bring the possibility of failure.

It's not the prospect of being part of a new and better firm that threatens people; it's the fear that they will not be able to keep up—the fear of failing, making mistakes or, even worse, not being good enough to be part of the new enterprise. It is critical, therefore, for the firm's leadership to be fully cognizant of this very destructive mind-set and actively work to overcome it. One way is to cultivate a new way of looking at mistakes.

Success and Failure

No one accomplishes something great without making mistakes in the process. The path to success is, more often than not, *laden* with mistakes. You cannot have success without experiencing failure.

Every part of the firm's leadership must develop and communicate an attitude of active tolerance toward mistakes. In law firms in particular (where people thrive on being right and, of course, on winning), there can be a real and palpable *intolerance* to making mistakes to the point that being wrong is considered shameful. This mind-set often destroys the greatest of efforts, and it is the single most challenging barrier for your firm to remove.

In building a firm—or any enterprise—mistakes will happen. They *must* happen. What must be discouraged, however, is people hiding their mistakes and not sharing what they have learned. Mistakes often produce valuable insights, and discovering these insights sometimes brings people together. Sharing what they've learned from mistakes can keep moving people forward and encourage risk taking. It is the foundation from which people take personal initiative. Without accepting—indeed, embracing—the risk of failure, people won't try new ways of doing things—new ways of being.

The Japanese have a keen understanding of the organizational process and give credit for success and responsibility for failure not to the individual, but to the group at large—they have a collective sense of accomplishment.

We must also acknowledge the element of luck in success and failure: Sometimes whether people succeed or fail has nothing to do with their actions, but with the collective forces that surround them. Of course, the possibility that luck had a hand in their success is not something people like to acknowledge.

A Funny Thing about Success…

Conventional thinking says that we become more productive when we experience success than when we experience failure. However, this is not always the case—especially when it comes to finding motivation. For many people, motivation comes from first being struck by what we think we *can't* do, then driven by our perseverance to overcome it.

Consider what country music legend Willie Nelson said about success. In a 1992 interview, he shared what he believed was the worst thing that had ever happened to him as a recording artist: his own success. With success, he said, fear sets in. You're not willing to risk making mistakes for fear of losing that success. What slowly disappeared, he observed, was his need to keep trying new ways of performing, breaking through old barriers and learning from his mistakes.

This is not to suggest that continued failure is particularly encouraging or productive—it's not. But neither is holding on to success so tightly that you stop taking risks for fear of losing it. This is why, after people succeed, they often stop trying anything new and spend the rest of their career living off their past victories. This happens in many fields and happens particularly often in large organizations.

In *Management of the Absurd*, Robert Tannenbaum writes, "Too many senior managers who may have been at the job for thirty years don't necessarily have thirty years of experience—they have more like one year of experience, thirty times." This is what happens when people get trapped in their own success.

Indeed, a great paradox is that success and failure are both illusions born of our need to think of life in absolute terms. People *like* winners, but they *relate* more to those who falter—those who struggle and fall only to get up and do it again.

Gore Vidal once said, "Whenever a friend succeeds, a little something in me dies"—a brutal but insightful bit of candor for us to ponder.

Finding Success Is about Our Mind-Sets

Achieving success is best viewed as a process, with failing simply one of the steps on the path toward succeeding. Thinking of success as a process makes us look at challenges in different ways. One way is to understand that fostering change requires patience: We have not failed; we have merely not yet succeeded.

Be realistic about your firm's expectations. You are out to reinvent the firm. Group transformation rarely occurs through conventional means. It must begin by those at the top giving the people around and below them the room to dream and see their own challenges within the context of the firm. Because people have different perspectives, leadership must be willing to broaden the scope of what's really possible as a result of such change. The goal is to invite others to participate in the firm's vision through their own vision; to let them express their feelings and thoughts; to encourage them to feel and express their dreams. This requires a new mind-set, and when it happens, contributions to the firm sometimes come from the most unexpected places.

To change the firm's mind-set, the core leadership needs to reexamine how it thinks about things such as diversity and group participation. It needs to reconsider what it assumes to be true about conventional wisdom. If the existing firm rejects out of hand such approaches, leadership must determine whether it can shift perspective and work differently.

Fighting Complacency

Until the firm's vision becomes the norm—built from the shared and accepted values of the firm—it will be subject to erosion. This is why the firm needs a strong and unrelenting coalition. The changes made must become embedded in the firm's way of doing business.

The key is to not let complacency set in. Your inner circle must take the lead with its respective teams (more on teams later in this chapter). Leaders must take the time to make sure each team member understands how your new approaches will add value to the firm and to them—how the changes will increase individual and collective productivity. This *must* be made clear. Don't assume that people will connect the dots on their own. They must be shown, then told, then shown again.

Some people, no matter what, will resist change. They fear change will bring about carnage—specifically, their own. They will work behind the scenes to manipulate sentiment, foster conflict, hide out and—when things get tough—bail out. This is not necessarily a bad thing. In fact, it can be a sign that fundamental change is upon the firm. These are exactly the types of people who need to leave the firm.

Knowing when someone doesn't fit into the vision is just as important as inspiring others to be part of the firm's vision, and, interestingly, can be just as inspiring. Think of the firm as a big bushy tree in need of trimming. The beauty emerges from its pruning. The leader knows this intuitively and does not hesitate to encourage people to move on when it becomes clear there is not a match.

Keep the Firm Energized

People feel energized when they see themselves as part of something larger than they are—part of a clear future, joined with others under a single mission. This can not only be inspiring, but can also bring out the best in everyone involved. Great leaders are naturals at fostering this energy in others. They can inspire others by showing them how their dreams can be concretely realized in the context of the firm's dreams. This *alignment* of interests is what generates and sustains forward-moving energy. Contrary to what most of us believe, dreaming is a good thing—even in the company of lawyers. It is no coincidence that, throughout history, those who were the biggest dreamers were also the biggest doers.

Grow Leadership

It should now be evident that fostering change requires committed leadership. How far the firm goes in reaching new and higher levels of performance will depend on how well it develops leadership skills in others. The first step in this process is to understand how powerful leaders think and to emulate their thinking.

Giving a talented managing partner time to manage is essential. The managing partner is just one person. He is limited to his individual capacity. Without strong teams headed by strong leaders, it is easy for managers to get bogged down in details and collapse under their weight.

A group's capacity is much greater, however. Managing other managers almost always brings exponential results, but it requires team management and leadership skills not readily found in most managing partners.

Firms with a hundred or more attorneys will unquestionably need a management system based on team leaders reporting directly to key partners, who, in turn, report to the managing partner and executive committee.

The firm must focus on knowledge distribution. This means organizing practice areas and administrative functions into discrete teams and subteams. The challenge is to give teams enough independence to be flexible while ensuring that their results are measured against the firm's vision.

Using teams allows leaders to delegate work and responsibility. A good leader pushes people to capacity, then coaches them past barriers. Surprisingly, studies show that people are most engaged—and most satisfied in their work—when they are challenged by learning new ways to work and when they are able to surpass old limits. In the process, important new skills and experiences are acquired. One such skill is learning how to work through teams.

Once they've worked under a strong leader, some people will seek to become leaders themselves. By observing and working with a strong team leader, they learn to emulate the leader's behavior; then they will test their new skills and develop their own leadership style. This is one of the great advantages of working in teams: It breeds new leaders who, in turn, breed more leaders.

Consistently building leadership skills throughout the firm is one of the most powerful ways of ensuring your firm's growth and prosperity.

Effectively managing team leaders who are held fully accountable for specific firm goals can be enormously productive—assuming, of course, that the team leaders are also given time to coach and counsel their respective team members.

Creating Leadership Teams

Every major practice group and department should be broken down into leadership teams. Determining the composition of each team will take thought and preparation. Ideally, teams will have no more than six members, because studies suggest that team momentum and effectiveness occur in small groups. Each team must include a strong leader, preferably someone with political clout at the firm—at a minimum, someone who is well respected by the team's peers. The team leader must be able to create a sense of urgency among team members and know how to collectively reward the team for obtaining results.

Working in teams is a way to open the firm to new possibilities because it has the unique element of *diversity*. Like all creative processes, teamwork can be unpredictable and open-ended. For some lawyers, working this way is difficult. The notion of accepting and, indeed, embracing open-ended and unpredictable results goes against a lawyer's fundamental training and safety zone.

It's been said that lawyers are like hermits, wanting to be left alone to do their job in the safety of their own isolation. This mind-set will hold your firm back and cause frustration in your efforts to create a team-based environment.

Team thinking begins with the acknowledgment that people gain more insight and results as a group than they do as individuals. An idea or expression may come from anyone on the team. The whole of the team is greater than the sum of its parts. This is especially true when the parts become fully integrated and work together to problem-solve.

Creative thinking, however, might come as a challenge for some lawyers. Their propensity is to be deeply analytical, logical and left-hemisphere-oriented. This is why firms should make sure that teams are composed of diverse types of employees.

Experienced team leaders know intuitively that diversity is a plus, and they value the *differences* in team members. In fact, teams that bear the greatest fruit are those that contain a mixed bag of people with differing mental, emotional, psychological and intellectual states.

No matter what the specific purpose of a team is—whether it's finding new ways of reducing administrative costs or identifying new practice areas—the results of its work must not only revolve around that purpose, but must also be measured against the firm's master charter. Ideally, the result will improve the quality of the relationship between the firm and the clients it serves. This responsibility must, in the end, rest with each of the team leaders.

Teams and Technology

As a facilitator, I work with firms to create a union between a firm's strategic vision and its intelligent use of technology. Technology, if thoughtfully designed, can be made to emulate the firm's strategic intentions. It can have the effect of binding with the firm's people and resources in ways that can create new levels of performance and opportunity.

Teams should work together at all levels, and clarity of purpose must be manifested in the firm's organizational design. Just as the firm's internal telephone directory lists lawyers, staff and departments, it should also list the firm's teams—their purposes, their leadership and their members.

When the firm removes the fuzziness and communication limitations inherent in large organizations, people have a way of becoming more accountable. By allowing everyone to know who is accountable for obtaining which results, no one is able to hide under the collective radar of the firm.

Knowing that others know what is expected of them creates an enormous incentive to fulfill individual obligations or face the consequences of letting the rest of the firm down—which, because of human nature, is not only embarrassing, it's avoided. Group pressure moves people into action.

I have seen firms reach truly unbelievable heights by exploiting the relational power of their own intranet. With the right planning and design, it permits and encourages team members to communicate not only among themselves and with others closely related to their team's purpose, but also with members of different types of teams.

If a firm is organized well, a snapshot of the firm's internal site map will reflect the structural essence of its communication paths, its action plans and its fundamental purpose. The site map becomes, in a sense, a living road map—an electronic portrait of the firm in action. Harnessing technology means being able to exploit its natural fluidity. Making changes to intranet structure is both inexpensive and fast.

The strategic use of technology to support change and achieve higher levels of communication can bring extraordinary results. People in the firm, and especially those who make up its teams, can see in real time how their own participation within the firm relates to and serves the collective benefit of the firm.

The next generation of "smart technology" will use both intranets and the Internet in such a way that clients, if they so choose, can fully participate in the firm's communication and information resources. Clients and firm members will be able to become part of the same paperless matrix. While most of the technology necessary to accomplish this already exists, what is painfully absent is our willingness to exploit its benefits fully and to stop clinging to our old ways of doing things.

12

Counselor-at-Law

The obligation of the legal profession is… to serve as healers of human conflict… [W]e should provide mechanisms that can produce an acceptable result in the shortest possible time, with the least possible expense and with a minimum of stress to the participants…

—*U.S. SUPREME COURT JUSTICE*
   WARREN BURGER

The term *counselor-at-law* is more in keeping with high goals and ambitions than the term *lawyer*. *Counselor* elicits an image of one who has deep knowledge—who dutifully informs and offers insight into critical matters of the mind and heart. A counselor is a person who guides others— a confidant and a pathfinder, and law firms would be wise to find ways to show their clients that they are *counselors* as well as *lawyers*.

Creating a change in image does not mean rejecting traditions that have contributed to a firm's past success. We must be careful not to toss out the proverbial baby with the bathwater. We should not take for granted the hard-won wisdom of the old traditions. The process of reinventing tradition need not always be at the expense of the past.

Progress is being made in the legal profession. Today, the art of mediation is being taught to lawyers in record numbers. Lawyers are seeing the value of keeping clients out of court and even experimenting with new methods of managing conflict resolution—sometimes on their own, but usually with the help of trained mediators.

Although the practice is still rare, lawyers are increasingly taking it upon themselves to meet with opposing counsel and discuss pathways to resolution for their respective clients.

Lawyers are beginning to see themselves as expert negotiators—as facilitators who are skilled at managing conflict proactively and helping parties to achieve mutual gain. This type of "counselor-to-counselor" mediation may be the beginning of a new tradition—one in which using the term *counselor-at-law* seems more appropriate.

"Counselors" are still advocates who must vigorously serve their clients' will in an adversarial forum. Yet we must remember that in days gone by, the court was considered a forum of truly last resort. Going to court often represented the failure of parties to resolve a dispute between themselves. The prospect of having strangers sit in judgment of one's personal affairs was considered embarrassing. It meant that the parties were not able to handle their affairs responsibly on their own but needed outside help.

Although some lawyers are turning to negotiation rather than lawsuits, legal education has not kept pace with the profound need to teach client communication skills to law students. Many law schools do not offer courses in management and leadership, negotiation and alternative dispute resolution or, in a more general context, how to serve clients well. Less than 10 percent of the law schools in this country offer even a single course on client communication skills, negotiation or even alternative dispute resolution.

Blind Advocacy

Law schools still believe that their role is to prepare students to become warriors; rarely are students taught that they may also be agents of resolution. To legal educators, the term *advocate* has traditionally been defined within the singular context of litigation. Lawyers, however, can also be advocates when they work toward resolution and finding ways to better serve their clients.

It is no surprise that law school graduates go on to become paper soldiers in a world filled with adversaries. The plaintiff is *adverse* to the defendant; the defendant is *adverse* to the plaintiff. Students are even taught how to protect themselves against their own clients. We lawyers measure ourselves by the number of wins we post, not by how skillfully we serve our clients' interests.

Lawyers are steeped in their adversarial domain, and this tradition is hard to change. Too often we see our roles as extensions of our clients' anger and frustration. We are like professional gladiators, wielding sword and shield, blazing a path to justice at almost any cost—even if we end up adding fuel to the fire and assuming greater levels of risk for our clients.

For new law-school graduates, the adversarial system must seem like a giant game station with its own set of rules—checks and balances. Each side is given equal access and the opportunity to use whatever traps and tricks they wish, with the assumption that in the end, justice will prevail. Students begin to think of themselves as hired guns—paid to win, but not necessarily paid to serve.

Today, trial advocacy is probably the single most popular elective taken in law school. Schools send their best and brightest students to compete nationally in the art of trial advocacy. Yet there is no national competition for serving clients well or negotiating and resolving difficult conflicts. At this time we can only imagine a competition where students win points for formulating creative strategies in negotiating a settlement or for demonstrating calm and reason at the negotiation table.

There's no doubt that going to battle releases more adrenaline than providing service. But does teaching our law-school students only one way of problem solving really provide them with a complete view of their future roles as lawyers and counselors?

Negotiating a case to settlement is not always the answer—there are legitimate reasons to settle matters in a courtroom rather than a mediator's office. Nonjudicial resolution may be impossible when the parties rightfully and legitimately want to have their day in court. Under these circumstances, what is the lawyer's role in the context of being a service-driven counselor?

The lawyer, as counselor, helps clients to identify and clarify priorities and to distinguish anger from reason. The lawyer makes sure that a client's decision to fight comes from a clear head and, if possible, that it is an unambiguous choice. In this counseling role, the lawyer helps a client to make a considered, thoughtful decision, born of free will, after all of the options have been explored and after all the costs and risks have been examined. Finally, when it is time for trial, the advocate skillfully and masterfully gives voice to and goes to battle for the client's cause.

How to Achieve a Good Lawyer-Client Relationship

In courting clients, a good rainmaker discovers the nature of a potential client's business and the specific challenges the person faces. When appropriate, the lawyer also learns as much as possible about the client personally.

This high level of commitment is the essence of being a fiduciary, and it does not end when the prospect becomes a client. Instead, taking on a new client must mark the beginning of a committed and conscious effort to serve.

For most lawyers, learning how to serve requires specific skill development and training. It requires learning the arts of listening and asking questions. These are the most undervalued and overlooked skills in the legal profession today. Law firms usually balk at investing in the education and professional development of their associates, and mentoring is often limited to developing legal skills, but developing communication and character skills should be at least equally as important.

Learning how to serve clients, especially for young associates, should not be a hit-and-miss process. Firms must take an active and determined stand regarding developing and sustaining a high level of communication skills throughout the firm. Promoting these skills should be as important as developing an associate's writing skills.

What Does It Mean for Clients to Count on Their Lawyers?

Action that arises from character is authentic and, therefore, predictable. Clients should find that their lawyers can be counted on under almost any circumstances. Lawyers who can be counted on to be responsible, attentive, caring, sensible, honest, hardworking and trustworthy will attract new clients and keep existing ones.

Developing a law firm driven by such inspired values will create growth and prosperity. These values cannot be imposed from the outside and cannot simply be words in the firm's brochure—they must originate at the core of the firm and grow outward. This is the essence of great marketing.

Justifying our hourly rates should have more to do with the service we deliver than the prevailing rate of the marketplace. The value of an extraordinary counselor—a trusted friend—is greater than one can imagine, and clients expect to pay more for such service. This is why, in the long run, no investment will bear greater returns than the investment firms make in marketing programs that reach into the essence of a firm and build service development systems that clients want and value inside and ask what it was that we really wanted and what it would take to get it.

Marketing ourselves is much more than promotion. It involves a search for professional identity. It must necessarily include, for each of us, an inquiry into our personal identity and then into the collective identity of the firm.

A concept such as finding our personal and collective identities may not be what you'd expect from a book on marketing—but it goes to the essence of how we really attract and keep new clients. Changing the way you market your firm will require a willingness to change your perceptions, leave the comfort of your domain and dare to imagine how things might be. Your new vision will be the catalyst for your success. It will align your firm with its highest values and distinguish it from other firms.

This strategy goes far beyond the conventional approach to marketing. It is based on strength of character, and the marketing that emerges from character will continually generate powerful opportunities for your firm. If you dare to consider what it might mean to find your unique voice as a professional and your own special brand of service, you will be infinitely rewarded.

Epilogue

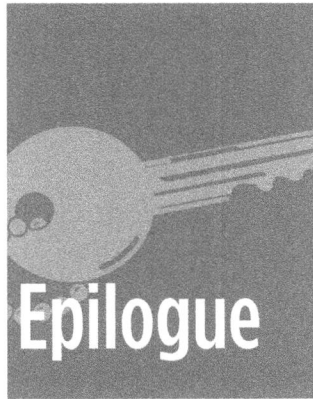

The ideas and goals presented here are not what readers might expect from a book about law firm marketing and management, yet the quality of our professional lives has a tremendous bearing on our personal lives and vice versa. Our professional lives are very much a part of who we are, and we are faced with the challenge of defining for ourselves the degree to which our professional lives give us meaning and purpose. Will we choose a professional life that is inspiring and engaging, dull and anxious, or somewhere in between?

Contrary to what most people believe, being truly satisfied in one's chosen profession does not simply happen. It is intentional, and it results from being committed to a process aimed at finding the goals and values that inspire us. Is this really part of marketing? It *is* marketing, for who we are as people is exactly what our clients see when they choose to retain us.

The basic difference between a great marketer and an ordinary one is that the great marketer sees the world as a series of inspiring challenges, while the ordinary one sees it as one unpleasant barrier after another. This is why ordinary marketing often brings ordinary results.

For many firms, marketing is concentrated on the pursuit of wealth and status. Unfortunately, such pursuit often devolves into nothing more than a mindless scramble for new clients without regard to the greater aims of the firm. Somehow values like integrity, honesty and compassion are lost, leaving the firm somewhere between hope and disillusionment.

Without leaders to chart a course driven by values that inspire and cultivate personal and professional growth, there can be no development of a firm character or a higher sense of purpose that will encourage members of the firm to move beyond their own needs and limits.

Most firms still see workers as units of production. As a result, workers at almost all levels are pigeonholed into narrowly defined positions. Rarely are firms concerned about how to tailor a job to bring out the *best* in their workers; instead, the emphasis is on how to get the *most* out of workers.

In the final analysis, people want to work for a cause, not just for a living. When work is exchanged for a paycheck and nothing more, sooner or later apathy sets in and workers put forth only the effort necessary to maintain their status in the firm.

Both lawyers and staff must be given the space to find meaning in their job—and finding this meaning almost always requires them to understand clearly how their personal and professional life can benefit from their relationship with the firm. People want to have their *own* inspired vision of their future, and how to make this vision possible within the context of the firm's vision is one of the major challenges facing law firms today.

Specifically, how does a firm create an environment that attracts and retains bright, enthusiastic and enterprising people? The first step is to acknowledge that most people seek positions that will expand their opportunities and encourage their personal and professional growth.

Firms that can provide such an environment will be able to hire—and keep—exceptionally capable and enterprising people. Doing this should be a firm's real goal. Nothing is more important to a law firm than constituting itself with talented and enthusiastic human capital. Impressive client lists, astute public relations and handsome brochures are no match for a firm that is made up of great and talented people. The profession of law is a profession of people first and foremost.

Reaching new levels of personal and professional satisfaction means knowing that you are truly doing and being your best while at the same time knowing that you are contributing to something greater than yourself.

Leadership is not something that is automatically funneled down through the ranks. A conscious and purposeful effort must be maintained to keep it cultivated and growing. Unfortunately, for most firms, staff and support positions can be so dull and uninspiring that doing one's best still means using a fraction of one's potential. This type of environment is unhealthy and will eventually temper even the most ambitious personalities at the firm.

We are all born with an assortment of aptitudes, many of which we are not even aware of having. The process of reinvention at the organizational level requires that we employ the full complement of our talents so that innovation and growth are embedded into every layer of the firm.

One New York partner told us what he thought was wrong with the way most firms go about filling positions:

> Our firm has been around for almost a hundred years. People come to work believing that the partners have designed this firm so that it all works in a special way, so its parts fit together to neatly produce what we call our firm's work product. Nothing could be further from the truth. No one person here, or for that matter, even groups of people at a firm, can see the whole. In filling positions, firms often ask their job applicants whether they have the talents and skillset to shape themselves around the demands and structure of the firm. I believe this approach can be a mistake. I think we ought to be asking prospective employees, "What can you bring to this firm that might help us to do a better job for our clients?" Not, "Here's the job description, just go follow it."

There will always be skeptics—those who run from new ideas and believe that the pursuit of personal and professional growth is simply too lofty a goal to consider or too soft a proposition to accurately measure. Some of these skeptics are immature and narcissistic, but they may be highly successful in environments where cunning and winning are highly valued; they may even attract loyalty from others because in the presence of such overbearing personalities, people believe they must follow or risk being fired. But deep inside, even those who follow such people are not fooled by such antics.

Unfortunately, blind allegiance is generally welcomed in highly structured environments such as big firms. But in this rapidly changing profession, much more is needed if the firm is to successfully compete and reach new levels of performance.

Lawyers, like most knowledge workers, require a degree of autonomy and the chance to pursue personal and professional development. Firms must be willing to accept—indeed, encourage—intellectual diversity and individualism. In the firm's mix of lawyers, some will be independent, others will be loners and still others will be conformists. Whatever the composition of the firm, if it is to succeed, the leadership and its culture must encourage everyone to reach higher and more meaningful levels of personal and professional growth.

In this way, marketing can be viewed as the total process by which the firm freely and intelligently chooses what it will ultimately become. And in doing so, the firm will be able to consistently turn its perspectives into powerful opportunities.

Afterword

We as human beings are living in a time of great change, and it can be seen and felt at every level of our society. Pushed ever forward by the forces of evolution, many of us are sensing that something deep within is beginning to emerge—a perception that exists beyond the ego and beyond its self-serving obsession with materialism and status.

I believe there is a transformative change happening at the level of our inner-most being. That we are entering a new paradigm—one in which our strength is measured by how successful we are in establishing caring and symbiotic relationships in every aspect of our personal, professional and social lives. It is a paradigm shift that values unity over division, peace over conquest.

We as lawyers have the opportunity, indeed the responsibility, to play a valuable and constructive role in this transformative process. And, within this process, we finally have the chance to redefine our profession. I speak of what Justice Berger referred to when he urged our profession to become "healers of human conflict."

I often wonder what it would be like professionally if we were viewed by the public as healers of conflict rather than perpetuators of conflict. I wonder what practicing law would look like and what values and choices we would make as healers. Perhaps we would choose values like union over division, inclusion over exclusion, and wisdom over cleverness.

Admittedly, it is not easy to think of the legal profession as being made up of healers. It takes some imagination, and yet personally, the very idea of it actually materializing in my lifetime or even in my children's lifetime deeply moves and inspires me.

To accomplish this we must move from a state of dreaming to a state of believing. To a state of living out the values we have chosen to embrace.

It dares us to be more than what we ever thought possible both personally and professionally.

The question is whether we shall lead the process of change or whether we shall lag behind it, still chained to those self-serving stale beliefs that no longer serve us as a society and which have kept us from realizing our greater potential as a profession.

I know where I stand on this issue. How about you?

Henry Dahut
San Francisco
henry@henrydahut.com

References, Resources and Recommendations

The books and articles listed below were used as resource material and represent an important foundation for many of the concepts presented in the book. I have also included a number of suggested readings and resources for your consideration.

Abell, Derek. *Defining the Business: Strategic Planning.*
    N.J. Prentice Hall, 1980.

Bazerman, Max. *Judgment in Managerial Decision Making.*
    New York: John Wiley & Sons, 2001.

Bennis, Warren. *On Becoming a Leader.*
    New York: Perseus Publishing, 2003.

Bennis, Warren. *The Secrets of Creative Collaboration.*
    New York: Perseus Publishing, 1998.

Bennis, Warren. Leaders: *The Strategies for Taking Charge.*
    Harper Business, 1997.

Caplan, Lincoln. *Power, Money, and the Rise of a Legal Empire.*
    Noonday Press, 1994.

Carter, Rita. *Mapping the Mind.*
    Berkeley: University of California Press, 1998.

Cathcart, Jim. *Relationship Selling.*
    New York: Putnam Publishing, 1990.

Chang, R. *The Passion Driven Organization.*
    San Francisco: Jossey-Bass, 2001.

Clark, Andy. *Putting Brain, Body, and World Together.*
    Cambridge: MIT Press, 1998.

Csikszentmihalyi, Mihaly. *Flow and the Psychology of Invention.*
New York: Harper 1997.

Damasio, Antonio. *The Making of Consciousness.*
New York: Harvest Books, 2000.

Drucker, Peter F. *"The New Productivity Challenge."*
Harvard Business Review 1969.

Gardner, Howard. *Leading Minds: An Anatomy of Leadership.*
New York: Basic Books, 1996.

Gerber, Michael E. *The E-Myth Revisited.*
New York: Harper Business, 1995.

Goleman, Daniel. *Emotional Intelligence.*
New York: Bantam, 1995.

Goleman, Daniel. *Primal Leadership: Emotional Intelligence.*
Boston: Harvard Press, 2002.

Gordan, Ian. *Relationship Marketing.*
New York: John Wiley & Sons, 1998.

Hart, Susan. *"Relationship Marketing and Legal Services."*
The Service Journal July 1998

Huttenlocher, Peter. *Neural Plasticity.*
Cambridge: Harvard University Press, 2002.

James, Jennifer. *Thinking in the Future Tense.*
New York: Simon & Schuster, 1996.

Katzenbach, Jon R. *The Wisdom of Teams.*
New York: Harper Business, 1994.

Keller, Kevin. *Strategic Brand Management.*
Upper Saddle River, N.J.: Prentice Hall, 1998.

Klein, Gary. *Sources of Power: How People Make Decisions.*
Cambridge: MIT Press, 1998.

Kotler, Philip. *Principles of Marketing.*
Saddle River, N.J. Prentice Hall, 2001.

LaBarre, Polly. *"Do You Have the Will to Lead?"*
Fast Company (March 2000)

Landsberg, Max. *The Tao of Coaching.*
New York: Harper Collins, 1997.

Leavitt, Theodore. *The Marketing Imagination.*
New York: Free Press, 1983.

Maister, David H. *Managing the Professional Service Firm.*
New York: Free Press, 1993.

Maister, David H. *The Trusted Advisor.*
New York: Free Press, 2000.

Maslow, Abraham. *Motivation and Personality.*
New York: Harper & Row, 1987.

Ogilvy, David. *On Advertising.*
New York: Vintage Books, 1983.

Ouchi, William. *Theory Z. Reading.*
Mass.: Addison-Wesley, 1981

Peters, Tom. *The Circle of Innovation.*
New York: Knopf, 1997.

Pinker, Stephen. *The Language Instinct.*
New York: HarperCollins, 1994.

Ratey, M.D., John J. *A User's Guide to the Brain.*
Cambridge: Harvard University Press, 1999.

Stewart, Thomas. *Intellectual Capital.*
New York: Doubleday, 1997.

Townsend, Robert. *Up the Organization.*
New York: Knopf, 1970.

Wilson, Edward. *The Unity of Knowledge.*
New York: Random House, 1998.

Wilson, Robert A. *"The Mind Beyond Itself."*
Oxford: Oxford University Press, 2000.

Zaltman, Gerald. *Theory Construction in Marketing.*
New York: John Wiley & Sons, 1982.

Index

L

M